Ultimate Soup & Sandwich Cookbook

Easy, Hearty & Delicious Meals For Everyday!

S. L. Watson

Copyright © 2019 S. L. Watson

All rights reserved.

ISBN: 9781712574607

No part of this book may be reproduced or utilized in any form or by any means, electronic or mechanical, including photocopying and recording without express written permission from the author and/or copyright holder. This book is for informational or entertainment purposes only. Cover design S. L. Watson 2019. Picture courtesy of Canva.

The author has made every effort to ensure the information provided in this book is correct. Failure to follow directions could result in a failed recipe. The author does not assume and hereby disclaim any liability to any party for any loss, damage, illness or disruption caused by errors and omissions, whether such errors and omissions result from negligence, accident or any other cause.

The author has made every effort to provide accurate information in the creation of this book. The author accepts no responsibility and gives no warranty for any damages or loss of any kind that might be incurred by the reader or user due to actions resulting from the use of the information in this book. The user assumes complete responsibility for the use of the information in this book.

DEDICATION

To everyone who loves a quick & delicious meal!

CONTENTS

	Introduction	i
1	Beef Soups & Sandwiches	1
2	Chicken & Turkey Soups & Sandwiches	33
3	Ham, Bacon & Pork Soups & Sandwiches	61
4	Egg & Cheese Soups & Sandwiches	102
5	Fish & Seafood Soups & Sandwiches	116
6	Meatless Soups & Sandwiches	139

INTRODUCTION

Soup & sandwich meals are an all time favorite. I have included numerous recipes for vegetable, meatless, beef, ground beef, chicken, turkey, seafood and bean soups along with the perfect sandwiches for your meal. If you love grilled cheese and BLT sandwiches, you will find numerous recipes for your favorites. Sandwiches include all your favorites plus a section for meatless sandwiches.

Don't think soups and sandwiches are just for the cold winter months. I have included cold sandwiches along with cold soups for those scorching summer days.

Soup & sandwich meals take the guess work out of What's For Dinner. For families with different schedules, most soups can be reheated and sandwiches made ahead or when ready to eat. If you don't have time to cook, there are plenty of fuss free soups and sandwiches that can be made in no time.

1 BEEF SOUPS & SANDWICHES

Beef soups and sandwiches are the most requested in my family. They are hearty and most are easy to make. Keep homemade soup on hand for cold winter days and during the holidays when company drops by for a warm meal.

Grilled Garlic Steak Sandwiches

Makes 4 sandwiches

1/2 tsp. dry mustard
1 1/2 tsp. garlic pepper seasoning
1 lb. boneless beef sirloin steak
1 large onion, peeled & cut into wedges
2 tsp. olive oil
2 tbs. unsalted butter, softened
4 hoagie buns, split
2 tbs. steak sauce
1 tomato, thinly sliced

In a small bowl, add the dry mustard and 1 teaspoon garlic pepper seasoning. Stir until combined and sprinkle over the steak. Have your grill hot and ready. Place the steak on the grill over medium coals or 350°. Cook for 4-5 minutes on each side or until the steak is done to your taste. Remove the steak from the grill and place on a plate. Let the steak rest for 8 minutes.

While the steak is cooking, place a small piece of aluminum foil on the grill. Add the onions to the aluminum foil. Brush the onion wedges with olive oil. Cook about 8-10 minutes or until the onions are tender. Remove from the grill.

In a small bowl, add 1/2 teaspoon garlic pepper seasoning and the butter. Stir until combined. Brush the butter on the cut sides of the buns. Place the buns, cut side down, on the grill. Cook for 2 minutes or until the buns are toasted. Remove the buns from the grill.

Cut the steak into thin slices. Spread the steak sauce on the cut sides of the buns. Place the steak over the bottom buns. Place the onions over the steak. Place the tomato slices over the top. Place the top on the sandwiches and serve.

Steak Stroganoff Sandwiches

Makes 4 servings

2/3 cup beer
1/3 cup vegetable oil
1 tsp. salt
1/4 tsp. garlic powder
Pinch of black pepper
2 lbs. flank steak
2 tbs. unsalted butter, melted
4 onions, thinly sliced
1/2 tsp. paprika
Pinch of salt
1 cup sour cream
1/2 tsp. prepared horseradish
8 slices French bread, toasted

In a shallow dish, add the beer, vegetable oil, 1 teaspoon salt, garlic powder and black pepper. Stir until well combined. Add the flank steak and turn the steak so both sides of the steak are coated in the marinade. Cover the dish and refrigerate for 8 hours.

Remove the steak from the refrigerator. Place the steak on a broiler pan. Turn the oven to the broiler position. Broil the steak for 5 minutes on each side or until the steak is cooked to your taste. Remove from the oven and let the steak rest for 5 minutes. Cut the steak, across the grain, into thin slices.

In a skillet over medium heat, add the butter, onions, paprika and pinch of salt. Saute for 6 minutes or until the onions are tender. Remove the skillet from the heat. In a microwavable bowl, add the sour cream and horseradish. Microwave for 30 seconds or until the sour cream is warm. Remove the bowl from the microwave and stir until combined.

Place the French bread slices on a serving platter. Spoon the steak and onions over the bread. Spoon the sour cream sauce over the top before serving.

Giant Meatball Sandwich

Makes 6 servings

1 lb. ground beef
1 lb. ground pork sausage
2 cups spaghetti sauce
1 garlic clove, minced
16 oz. loaf Italian bread
6 oz. sliced provolone cheese

In a mixing bowl, add the ground beef and sausage. Using your hands, mix until the meats are combined. Form the meat into 1" meatballs. In a skillet over medium heat, add the meatballs. Cook about 10 minutes or until the meatballs are well browned and no longer pink. Drain off the excess drippings. Remove the meatballs from the skillet and drain on paper towels.

Add the spaghetti sauce and garlic to the skillet. Saute the garlic for 2 minutes. Add the meatballs back to the skillet. Stir frequently and cook for 12 minutes. The meatballs should be tender. Remove the skillet from the heat.

Cut the bread in half lengthwise. Preheat the oven to the broiler position. Place the bread on a baking sheet. Broil for 3 minutes or until the bread is toasted. Remove the bread from the oven. Remove the bread from the bottom half of the loaf leaving about a 1/2" shell on the bread.

Spoon the meatballs and sauce into the bottom part of the loaf. Place the provolone cheese slices over the meatballs. Place the top half on the sandwich. Cut into wedges and serve.

Pizza Meatball Subs

Makes 6 servings

1 egg, beaten
1/3 cup steak sauce
1 cup crushed saltines
1 tsp. onion powder
1/4 tsp. season salt
1/8 tsp. black pepper
1 1/2 lbs. ground beef
6 tbs. mayonnaise
6 sub rolls, split
8 oz. American cheese slices, cut into thin strips
14 oz. jar pizza sauce
2 cups shredded mozzarella cheese

In a mixing bowl, add the egg, steak sauce, saltines, onion powder, season salt, black pepper and ground beef. Using your hands, mix until well combined. Form the meat into 1" meatballs.

Preheat the oven to 375°. Line a baking pan with aluminum foil. Place the meatballs on the pan. Bake for 25 minutes or until the meatballs are browned and no longer pink. Remove the pan from the oven and drain off the excess grease. Leave the oven on.

Spread 1 tablespoon mayonnaise on the bottom of each sub roll. Place the American cheese strips over the mayonnaise. Spread 1 tablespoon pizza sauce over the cheese on each sandwich. Spoon the meatballs over the cheese. Spoon the remaining pizza sauce over the meatballs. Sprinkle the mozzarella cheese over the meatballs.

Place the top on the rolls. Place the sandwiches on a large baking sheet. Bake for 10 minutes or until the cheese melts and the subs are hot. Remove from the oven and serve.

Meatloaf Sandwiches

Makes 4 servings

16 oz. loaf Italian bread
2 1/2 tbs. unsalted butter
1/2 cup chopped onion
1 cup sliced fresh mushrooms
1 egg
6 tbs. ketchup
1 1/2 cups shredded cheddar cheese
1 lb. lean ground beef
1/2 cup beef broth
1 tsp. garlic salt
1/4 tsp. dried thyme
3 tbs. mayonnaise

Cut the bread loaf in half lengthwise. Scoop out the inside of the bread leaving about a 1/4" shell on the bread halves. Place the scooped out bread in a mixing bowl. Tear the bread into small pieces. You need 1 1/2 cups breadcrumbs for this recipe. If you have more than 1 1/2 cups breadcrumbs, save the breadcrumbs for another recipe.

In a skillet over medium heat, add 1 1/2 tablespoons butter. When the butter melts, add the onion and mushrooms. Saute the vegetables for 5 minutes or until tender. Remove the skillet from the heat and add the onion and mushrooms to the bowl with the breadcrumbs. Add the egg, 3 tablespoons ketchup, 1/2 cup cheddar cheese, ground beef, beef broth, garlic salt and thyme to the bowl. Using your hands, mix until well combined.

Shape the meat into a 7" loaf and place on a baking sheet. Preheat the oven to 350°. Bake for 1 hour or until the meatloaf is browned and no longer pink. Remove the meatloaf from the oven but leave the oven on. Spread the mayonnaise over the bread halves. Place the meatloaf inside the bottom bread half. Spread 3 tablespoons ketchup over the meatloaf. Sprinkle 1 cup cheddar cheese over the meatloaf. Place the top half of bread over the sandwich.

Add 1 tablespoon butter to a small bowl. Microwave for 10 seconds or until the butter is melted. Brush the butter over the top half of bread. Wrap the loaf in aluminum foil. Bake for 15 minutes or until the bread is thoroughly heated. Remove the sandwich from the oven and carefully remove the aluminum foil. Cut the sandwich into wedges and serve.

Beef Stuffed Sourdough Sandwiches

Makes 8 servings

1 1/2 lbs. ground beef
1/2 cup chopped onion
15 oz. can tomato sauce
4 oz. can diced green chiles, drained
1/2 cup chopped fresh mushrooms
2 tbs. chili powder
2 tbs. sliced black olives
1/4 tsp. garlic salt
1 cup shredded cheddar cheese
8 sourdough rolls

In a skillet over medium heat, add the ground beef and onion. Stir frequently to break the ground beef into crumbles as it cooks. Cook for 8 minutes or until the ground beef is well browned and no longer pink. Drain off the excess grease.

Add the tomato sauce, green chiles, mushrooms, chili powder, black olives and garlic salt to the skillet. Stir until well combined. Reduce the heat to medium low. Stir occasionally and simmer for 10 minutes. Remove the skillet from the heat and stir in the cheddar cheese.

Cut a 1/4" slice off the top of each sourdough roll. Gently remove the bread from the bottom part leaving about a 1/4" shell on the bread. Use the removed bread for another recipe. Spoon the beef filling into the bottom shell. Place the top on the sandwiches.

You can wrap the sandwiches in aluminum foil at this point and freeze up to 3 months. Reheat thawed sandwiches in the oven for 25 minutes at 350° before serving or until the sandwiches are hot. Thaw the frozen sandwiches in the refrigerator.

To bake the sandwiches when prepared, place the sandwiches on a baking sheet. Preheat the oven to 350°. Bake for 10 minutes or until the sandwiches are toasted and hot. Remove from the oven and serve.

Cheeseburger Meatloaf Hoagies

Makes 8 sandwiches

1 egg, beaten
1 cup tomato sauce
1 cup quick cooking oats
1/4 cup chopped onion
1/2 tsp. salt
1/2 tsp. black pepper
1 1/2 lbs. ground beef
1/3 cup mayonnaise
2 tbs. ketchup
8 tomato slices
8 slices cheddar cheese, about 1 oz. each
8 bacon slices, cooked and halved
8 hoagie buns, split and toasted

In a mixing bowl, add the egg, tomato sauce, oats, onion, salt, black pepper and ground beef. Using your hands, mix until well combined. Press the meat into the bottom of a 9 x 13 baking dish.

Preheat the oven to 350°. Bake for 30 minutes or until the meatloaf is well browned and no longer pink. Remove the dish from the oven. Drain off any grease.

In a small bowl, add the mayonnaise and ketchup. Stir until combined and spread over the meatloaf. Cut the meatloaf into 8 rectangles. Place a tomato slice, cheddar cheese slice and bacon slice over each rectangle.

Turn the oven to the broiler position. Broil for 2 minutes or until the cheese melts. Remove the dish from the oven. Place a meatloaf slice on the bottom half of each hoagie bun. Place the top on the buns and serve.

Basil Tomato Meatloaf Sandwiches

Makes 8 sandwiches

1 1/2 lbs. lean ground beef
3/4 cup quick cooking oats
3/4 cup whole milk
1/4 cup chopped onion
1 egg, beaten
1 1/2 tsp. salt
1/4 tsp. black pepper
1/3 cup ketchup
2 tbs. light brown sugar
1 tbs. yellow prepared mustard
8 slices frozen Texas Toast garlic bread
1/2 cup mayonnaise
1 tbs. chopped fresh basil
1 cup shredded lettuce
2 plum tomatoes, sliced

In a mixing bowl, add the ground beef, oats, milk, onion, egg, salt and black pepper. Using your hands, mix until combined. Pat the meat into a 9 x 5 loaf pan. In a small bowl, add the ketchup, brown sugar and mustard. Stir until combined and spread over the meatloaf.

Preheat the oven to 350°. Bake for 1 hour or until the meatloaf is no longer pink. Remove the pan from the oven and drain off any excess grease. Cool the meatloaf for 10 minutes.

Place the garlic bread on a baking sheet. Bake for 8 minutes or until the bread is golden brown. Remove the bread from the oven. In a small bowl, add the mayonnaise and basil. Stir until combined and spread on one side of each piece of garlic bread. Sprinkle the lettuce over mayonnaise. Place the tomatoes over the lettuce. Cut the meatloaf into 8 slices. Place a slice over each bread slice and serve.

Marinated Steak Sandwiches

Makes 6 sandwiches

1 cup dry red wine
3 tbs. soy sauce
1 tbs. minced garlic
1/8 tsp. black pepper
2 flank steaks, 1 lb. each
2 tbs. olive oil
6 slices frozen Texas Toast garlic bread
2 cups diced tomatoes
3 cups chopped lettuce

In a Ziploc bag, add the red wine, soy sauce, garlic, black pepper and flank steaks. Close the bag and shake until the marinade is combined and the steaks are coated in the marinade. Refrigerate the steaks at least 2 hours but not more than 12 hours.

Remove the steaks from the bag. Discard the marinade. In a skillet over medium high heat, add the olive oil. When the oil is hot, add the flank steaks. Cook for 3 minutes on each side or until the steaks are cooked to your taste. Remove the skillet from the heat. Let the steaks rest for 5 minutes.

Preheat the oven to 400°. Place the garlic bread slices on a baking sheet. Bake for 5 minutes or until the garlic bread is golden brown. Remove the pan from the oven.

Place the garlic bread slices on a serving platter. Thinly slice the steaks across the grain. Place the steak slices over the garlic bread. Sprinkle the tomatoes and lettuce over the top and serve.

Stromboli Sandwiches

Makes 8 servings

2 lbs. ground beef
1/4 cup finely chopped onion
1 cup ketchup
1 cup tomato sauce
1/4 cup grated Parmesan cheese
2 tsp. garlic powder
1 tsp. dried oregano
1/2 tsp. fennel seed
1/2 tsp. dried Italian seasoning
2 loaves Italian bread, 1 lb. size
1/2 cup unsalted butter, softened
2 cups shredded mozzarella cheese

In a dutch oven over medium heat, add the ground beef and onion. Stir frequently to break the ground beef into crumbles as it cooks. Cook for 10 minutes or until the ground beef is well browned and no longer pink. Drain off the excess grease.

Add the ketchup, tomato sauce, Parmesan cheese, 1/2 teaspoon garlic powder, oregano, fennel seed and Italian seasoning. Stir until combined and bring to a boil. Reduce the heat to medium low. Stir occasionally and simmer for 15 minutes or until the filling thickens. Remove the skillet from the heat.

Cut each Italian bread loaf in half lengthwise. In a small bowl, add the butter and 1 1/2 teaspoons garlic powder. Stir until combined and spread on the cut sides of the loaves. Sprinkle 1/4 cup mozzarella cheese over the butter on each piece.

Spoon the ground beef filling over the bottom bread halves. Sprinkle 1/2 cup mozzarella cheese over the ground beef on each loaf. Place the tops on the sandwiches. Wrap the sandwiches in aluminum foil.

Preheat the oven to 350°. Place the sandwiches on a baking pan. Bake for 25 minutes or until the sandwiches are hot and the cheese melted. Remove from the oven and cut into slices to serve.

Caramelized Onion Beef Sandwiches

Makes 4 sandwiches

1 tsp. salt
1/4 tsp. garlic powder
1/4 tsp. paprika
1/4 tsp. black pepper
1 lb. beef tenderloin
3 tbs. unsalted butter
1 tbs. vegetable oil
2 tbs. light brown sugar
3 onions, peeled and thinly sliced
2 tbs. water
8 slices frozen Texas Toast garlic bread
1 1/2 cups fresh baby spinach

Preheat the oven to 450°. In a small bowl, add 1/2 teaspoon salt, garlic powder, paprika and black pepper. Stir until combined and rub over the beef tenderloin. Place the beef tenderloin in a roasting pan. Bake for 30 minutes or until the tenderloin is done to your taste. Remove the tenderloin from the oven and cool while you prepare the onions. Leave the oven on.

In a large skillet over medium heat, add the butter and vegetable oil. When the oil is hot, add the brown sugar, 1/2 teaspoon salt, onions and water. Stir frequently and cook for 15 minutes. The onions should be lightly caramelized when ready. Remove the skillet from the heat.

While the onions are cooking, bake the garlic bread. Place the garlic bread slices on a baking sheet. Bake for 5-7 minutes or until the garlic bread is golden brown. Remove the garlic bread from the oven.

Thinly slice the beef tenderloin and place the slices over 4 garlic bread slices. Spoon the onions over the beef. Sprinkle the spinach over the onions. Place the remaining garlic bread slices over the sandwiches and serve.

Cheese Steak Melts

Makes 4 servings

16 oz. loaf frozen garlic bread, thawed
2 cups shredded mozzarella cheese
1 lb. thinly sliced deli roast beef
1 tsp. Montreal steak seasoning
1 1/2 cups thinly sliced onions
1 1/2 cups thinly sliced green bell peppers

Preheat the oven to 400°. Separate the garlic bread into halves. Place the garlic bread on a baking sheet. Sprinkle the mozzarella cheese over one garlic bread half. Place the roast beef slices over the cheese. Sprinkle the Montreal steak seasoning over the roast beef. Sprinkle the onions and green bell peppers over the roast beef. Place the remaining garlic bread half over the top of the sandwich.

Wrap the garlic bread in aluminum foil. Bake for 30 minutes or until the garlic bread is toasted and the onions and peppers tender. Remove the sandwich from the oven. Cut into slices and serve.

Cheesy Roast Beef Buns

Makes 6 servings

1 cup chopped onion
2 tbs. unsalted butter
8 oz. jar process cheese sauce
1 lb. cooked roast beef, thinly sliced
6 Italian sandwich buns

In a skillet over medium heat, add the onion and butter. Saute for 5 minutes. Add the cheese sauce to the skillet. Stir constantly and cook until the sauce is hot. Add the roast beef to the skillet. Stir until combined and remove the skillet from the heat.

Spoon the beef onto the bottom of the buns. Place the top on the sandwiches. Wrap each sandwich in aluminum foil and place on a baking sheet. Preheat the oven to 350°. Bake for 10 minutes. Remove the sandwiches from the oven and serve.

Horseradish Roast Beef Sandwiches

This is a great sandwich for leftover roast.

Makes 4 servings

3 oz. cream cheese, softened
2 tbs. mayonnaise
2 tbs. mango chutney
3 tsp. prepared horseradish
4 hoagie rolls, split & toasted
4 lettuce leaves
12 oz. thinly sliced cooked roast beef
2 tomatoes, thinly sliced
6 mozzarella cheese slices, 1 oz. size
4 thin purple onion slices
Black pepper to taste

In a small bowl, add the cream cheese, mayonnaise, mango chutney and horseradish. Stir until combined and spread on the cut sides of the hoagie buns. Place a lettuce leaf on the bottom of the rolls. Place the roast beef over the lettuce.

Place the tomatoes over the roast beef. Place a mozzarella cheese slice and a purple onion slice over the tomatoes. Season to taste with black pepper. Place the top roll on the sandwiches and serve.

Roast Beef BLT

Makes 4 servings

12 oz. loaf focaccia bread
1/2 cup mayonnaise
1 tsp. prepared horseradish
3 lettuce leaves
1 lb. cooked roast beef, thinly sliced
6 bacon slices, cooked
8 fresh tomato slices

Cut the focaccia bread in half horizontally. In a small bowl, add the mayonnaise and horseradish. Stir until combined and spread on the cut sides of the bread. Place the lettuce over the bottom loaf. Place the roast beef over the lettuce. Place the bacon and tomatoes over the roast beef. Place the top on the sandwich. Cut into slices and serve.

Hot Beef Sandwiches With Au Jus

Makes 16 sandwiches

5 lb. beef rump roast
1 envelope dry onion soup mix
2 tsp. granulated sugar
1 tsp. dried oregano
2 cans condensed beef broth, 10 oz. size
12 oz. can beer
2 garlic cloves, minced
16 crusty French rolls, halved lengthwise

Preheat the oven to 300°. In a dutch oven, add the beef roast. In a mixing bowl, add the onion soup mix, granulated sugar, oregano, beef broth, beer and garlic. Whisk until combined and pour over the roast. Place a lid on the pan.

Bake for 5 hours or until the roast is tender enough to shred. Remove the roast from the oven. Let the roast rest for 15 minutes. Shred the roast using two forks.

Spoon the roast onto the bottom French rolls. Skim the fat from the pan juices and serve with the sandwiches.

Round Steak Sandwiches

Makes 6 servings

3 large onions, peeled & thinly sliced
3 tbs. melted unsalted butter
1 tbs. garlic oil
1 1/4 lb. round steak, cut into wafer thin slices
6 hoagie rolls, toasted
1/2 cup picante sauce

In a large skillet over medium high heat, add the onions and butter. Saute for 10 minutes or until the onions are golden brown. Remove the onions from the skillet and drain on paper towels.

Add the garlic oil to the skillet. When the oil is hot, add the round steak. Saute for 5 minutes or until the steak slices are well browned. Remove the skillet from the heat.

Place the steak on the bottom rolls. Spoon the onions over the steak. Drizzle the picante sauce over the onions. Place the top on the sandwiches and serve.

Salt Roasted Beef Tenderloin Sliders With Chimichurri Pesto

Makes 8 servings

1 1/2 lb. beef tenderloin, trimmed
1 tsp. black pepper
1 tbs. olive oil
6 cups kosher salt
1 cup cold water
1 cup fresh parsley
1 cup fresh cilantro leaves
1/2 cup chopped toasted walnuts
1/2 cup freshly grated Parmesan cheese
1 tsp. fresh lemon juice
1 garlic clove, minced
1/4 tsp. dried crushed red pepper flakes
1/4 tsp. salt
1/4 cup olive oil
24 slider buns, toasted

Sprinkle the black pepper over the beef tenderloin. In a skillet over medium high heat, add the olive oil. When the oil is hot, add the tenderloin. Cook for 3 minutes on each side or until well browned. Remove the skillet from the heat.

In a mixing bowl, add 6 cups kosher salt and cold water. Stir until combined. Pour half the salt into a roasting pan. Form the salt into a rectangle about 2" larger than the tenderloin. Place the beef tenderloin over the salt. Spoon the remaining salt over the tenderloin. Pat the salt to form around the tenderloin. The tenderloin should be totally covered in the salt.

Preheat the oven to 400°. Bake for 45 minutes or until a meat thermometer registers 150° in the thickest part of the tenderloin. Remove the pan from the oven. Using a wooden spoon, tap the salt to break the salt apart. Immediately remove the tenderloin from the salt and place on a serving platter. Loosely cover the tenderloin with aluminum foil. Let the tenderloin rest while you make the chimichurri pesto. The tenderloin needs to rest for 10 minutes.

In a food processor, add the parsley, cilantro, walnuts, Parmesan cheese, lemon juice, garlic, red pepper flakes and 1/4 teaspoon salt. Process until smooth and combined. With the food processor running, slowly add the olive oil. Process until well combined.

Cut the tenderloin into 24 thin slices and place on the buns. Spoon the chimichurri pesto over the beef. Place the top on the buns and serve.

Spicy Shredded Beef Sandwiches

Makes 6 servings

2 1/2 lb. boneless chuck roast, trimmed
14 oz. can diced tomatoes
7 oz. can adobo sauce
4 oz. can diced green chiles, drained
1 3/4 cups chopped onion
4 garlic cloves, minced
2 tbs. chili powder
1 tbs. honey
2 1/2 tsp. salt
1 tsp. ground cumin
2 cups beef broth
6 large crusty rolls

Add the roast to a 5 quart slow cooker. In a mixing bowl, add the tomatoes with juice, adobo sauce, green chiles, onion, garlic, chili powder, honey, salt, cumin and beef broth. Whisk until combined and pour over the roast.

Set the temperature to high and cook for 1 hour. Reduce the temperature to low. Cook for 8 hours or until the roast is tender enough to shred. Remove the roast from the slow cooker. Remove half the sauce and place in a bowl. Add the roast back to the slow cooker. Shred the roast using two forks. Stir until the roast is combined with the sauce left in the slow cooker.

Cut the rolls in half and place the bottoms on a serving platter. Spoon the roast over the rolls. Place the top half of the rolls on the sandwiches. Serve with the reserved sauce.

Smothered Beef Sandwiches

Makes 6 sandwiches

16 oz. loaf frozen garlic bread, thawed
3 cups cooked diced roast beef
1/2 cup barbecue sauce
1 1/2 cups shredded American cheese

Preheat the oven to 375°. Separate the garlic bread into halves. In a small bowl, add the roast beef and barbecue sauce. Stir until combined and spoon over the garlic bread. Bake for 10 minutes or until the garlic bread is toasted. Sprinkle the American cheese over the top. Bake for 5 minutes or until the cheese melts. Remove the garlic bread from the oven. Cut into slices and serve.

Cheddar French Dip Sandwiches

Makes 4 servings

1/4 cup unsalted butter, cubed
2 garlic cloves, minced
4 ciabatta rolls, split
1 cup shredded cheddar cheese
1 lb. thinly sliced cooked roast beef
14 oz. can beef broth

In a small skillet over medium heat, add the butter. When the butter melts, add the garlic. Saute for 1 minute. Remove the skillet from the heat. Brush the cut sides of the ciabatta rolls with the garlic butter. Place the rolls on a baking sheet.

Preheat the oven to the broiler position. Sprinkle the cheddar cheese over the top of the rolls. Broil for 3 minutes or until the rolls are toasted and the cheese melts. Remove the rolls from the oven.

While the rolls are baking, add the roast beef and beef broth to a sauce pan over medium heat. Stir constantly and cook about 5 minutes or until hot and bubbly. Remove the pan from the heat. Using a slotted spoon, remove the beef from the broth and place on the bottom rolls. Place the top on the sandwiches and serve with the remaining beef broth.

Beef Stroganoff Sandwiches

Makes 8 servings

1 1/2 lbs. ground beef
1 cup chopped onion
2 garlic cloves, minced
2 tbs. all purpose flour
1/2 tsp. salt
1/2 tsp. paprika
10.75 oz. can cream of mushroom soup
1/2 cup sliced fresh mushrooms
8 slices frozen Texas Toast garlic bread

In a skillet over medium heat, add the ground beef, onion and garlic. Stir frequently to break the ground beef into crumbles as it cooks. Cook for 8 minutes or until the ground beef is well browned and no longer pink. Drain off any excess grease.

Add the all purpose flour, salt and paprika to the skillet. Stir constantly and cook for 2 minutes. Add the cream of mushroom soup and mushrooms. Stir until combined and simmer for 5 minutes. The stroganoff should be hot and bubbly. Remove the skillet from the heat.

While the ground beef is cooking, bake the garlic bread. Preheat the oven to 400°. Place the garlic bread slices on a baking pan. Bake for 8 minutes or until the garlic bread is toasted and golden brown. Remove the garlic bread from the oven.

Place the garlic bread on a serving platter. Spoon the stroganoff over the top and serve.

Garlic Sloppy Joes

Makes 6 servings

1 lb. lean ground beef
1/2 cup chopped onion
1/2 cup chopped green bell pepper
14 oz. can fire roasted diced tomatoes with garlic
1/2 cup ketchup
1 tsp. chili powder
1 tsp. Worcestershire sauce
1/4 tsp. salt
1/8 tsp. black pepper
6 frozen Texas Toast garlic bread slices
6 slices provolone cheese, 1 oz. each

In a skillet over medium heat, add the ground beef, onion and green bell pepper. Stir frequently to break the ground beef into crumbles as it cooks. Cook for 10 minutes or until the ground beef is no longer pink and well browned. Drain off any grease from the ground beef.

Add the tomatoes with juice, ketchup, chili powder, Worcestershire sauce, salt and black pepper to the skillet. Stir constantly and cook for 5 minutes. Remove the skillet from the heat.

While the ground beef is cooking, bake the garlic bread. Preheat the oven to 400°. Place the garlic bread slices on a baking sheet. Bake for 7 minutes or until the garlic bread is golden brown and toasted. Remove from the oven. Spoon the ground beef over the garlic bread. Place a provolone cheese slice over each serving.

Turn the oven to the broiler position. Broil for 2 minutes or until the cheese is melted and bubbly. Remove the sandwiches from the oven and serve.

Ground Beef Reuben Melts

Makes 6 sandwiches

1 lb. lean ground beef
1/4 cup chopped onion
2 garlic cloves, minced
1 cup sauerkraut
1/2 cup prepared Thousand Island dressing
6 slices dark rye bread, toasted
6 slices Swiss cheese, 1 oz. size

In a skillet over medium heat, add the ground beef, onion and garlic. Stir frequently to break the ground beef into crumbles as it cooks. Cook for 8 minutes or until the ground beef is well browned and no longer pink. Remove the skillet from the heat and drain off the excess grease.

In a microwavable bowl, add the sauerkraut. Microwave for 1 minute or until the sauerkraut is hot. Remove the bowl from the microwave. Add the Thousand Island dressing to the ground beef.

Place the bread slices on a baking sheet. Spread the ground beef over the bread slices. Spoon the sauerkraut over the top. Place a Swiss cheese slice over the top of each sandwich. Turn the oven to the broiler position. Broil for 2 minutes or until the cheese melts and is bubbly. Remove from the oven and serve.

Spicy Coleslaw Reubens

Makes 6 sandwiches

10 oz. pkg. finely shredded cabbage
4 green onions, sliced
1 tsp. olive oil
1/2 cup Thousand Island dressing
3 tbs. spicy brown mustard
12 sourdough sandwich bread slices
6 slices Pepper Jack cheese
1 lb. thinly sliced corned beef

In a skillet over medium heat, add the cabbage, green onions and olive oil. Saute for 5 minutes or until the cabbage is tender. Remove the skillet from the heat and stir in the Thousand Island dressing. Spread the brown mustard over one side of each bread slice. Place the Pepper Jack cheese and corned beef over the brown mustard on 6 bread slices. Spoon the cabbage coleslaw over the top of the corned beef and cheese. Place the remaining slices over the sandwiches.

In a skillet over medium heat, add the sandwiches. Cook about 3 minutes per side or until the bread is toasted. Remove the skillet from the heat and serve.

Grilled Reubens With Homemade Dressing

Makes 6 servings

1 cup mayonnaise
1/2 cup chili sauce
3 tbs. pimento stuffed olives, chopped
1 tbs. chopped fresh parsley
1 tbs. diced red pimento
1 tbs. honey
1/2 tsp. lemon juice
1/4 tsp. onion powder
12 capers, rinsed & chopped
2 cups jarred sauerkraut, drained
3/4 tsp. caraway seeds
12 rye bread slices
6 slices pumpernickel bread
12 slices Swiss cheese, 1 oz. size
1 lb. corned beef, thinly sliced
2 tbs. softened unsalted butter

Add the mayonnaise, chili sauce, olives, parsley, red pimento, honey, lemon juice, onion powder and capers to a small bowl. Stir until combined. Cover the bowl and chill for 3 hours before serving.

In a mixing bowl, add the sauerkraut and caraway seeds. Stir until combined. Spread the dressing over one side of 6 rye bread slices. Spread the dressing over one side of the pumpernickel bread slices. Place 1 Swiss cheese slice over the dressing on each bread slice. Place half the sauerkraut and corned beef over the cheese on the rye bread slices.

Place the pumpernickel bread slices, dressing side down, over the corned beef. Spread the remaining sauerkraut and corned beef over the pumpernickel bread. Spread the remaining rye bread slices with the dressing on one side of the bread. Place the bread, dressing side down, over the corned beef.

Spread the butter on the outside bread slices. In a large skillet over medium heat, add the sandwiches. Cook about 4 minutes on each side or until hot, golden brown and the cheese melted. Remove the skillet from the heat and serve.

Garlic Bread Meatball Sandwiches

Makes 6 servings

1 onion, diced
1 green bell pepper, diced
1 tbs. olive oil
1 tbs. chopped fresh basil
32 oz. pkg. frozen cooked meatballs
26 oz. jar spaghetti sauce
6 slices French bread, about 1" thick
1/2 cup garlic butter
1 cup shredded Parmesan cheese
2 cups shredded mozzarella cheese

In a skillet over medium heat, add the onion, green bell pepper and olive oil. Saute the vegetables for 5 minutes. Add the basil, meatballs and spaghetti sauce. Stir frequently and cook for 30 minutes. Remove the skillet from the heat.

Spread the garlic butter on both sides of the French bread. Preheat the oven to 400°. Place the bread slices on the baking sheet. Bake for 6 minutes or until the bread is toasted. Remove the bread from the oven.

Place the bread on a serving platter. Spoon the meatballs and sauce over the bread. Sprinkle the Parmesan cheese and mozzarella cheese over the sandwiches and serve.

French Beef Sandwich

Makes 8 servings

1 lb. loaf French bread
1 lb. ground chuck
1 onion, chopped
10.75 oz. can condensed tomato soup
11 oz. can cheddar cheese soup

Cut the bread in half lengthwise. Remove the bread from the inside of the halves leaving about 1/2" shell on the bread. Break the removed bread into bite size pieces. In a skillet over medium heat, add the ground chuck and onion. Stir frequently to break the meat into crumbles as it cooks. Cook about 8 minutes or until the ground chuck is well browned and no longer pink. Drain off the excess grease.

Stir in the removed bread pieces, tomato soup and cheddar cheese soup. Stir until well combined. Cook only until the soups are thoroughly heated. Remove the skillet from the heat and spoon the meat into the bottom loaf of the bread. Place the top half of bread on the sandwich. Wrap the sandwich in aluminum foil. Preheat the oven to 350°. Bake for 30 minutes. Remove the sandwich from the oven and cut into slices before serving.

Taco Vegetable Soup

Makes 14 cups

1 lb. ground beef
2 cans rinsed & drained pinto beans, 15 oz. size
10 oz. pkg. frozen cut green beans
15 oz. can ranch beans
14 oz. can stewed tomatoes
14 oz. can petite diced tomatoes
10 oz. pkg. frozen whole kernel corn
1 1/2 cups chicken broth
1 envelope taco seasoning mix
1 oz. envelope dry ranch dressing mix

In a dutch oven over medium heat, add the ground beef. Stir frequently to break the ground beef into crumbles as it cooks. Cook for 8 minutes or until the ground beef is well browned and no longer pink. Drain the grease from the pan.

Add the pinto beans, green beans, ranch beans with sauce, tomatoes with juice, corn, chicken broth, taco seasoning and ranch dressing mix to the pan. Stir constantly and bring to a boil. Reduce the heat to medium low. Stir occasionally and simmer for 30 minutes. Remove the pan from the heat and serve.

Perfect with Pepper Jack Cheese Sandwiches.

Meatless option: Omit the ground beef or use 1 cup Grillers crumbles in place of the ground beef. Substitute vegetable broth for the chicken broth.

Taco Minestrone

This is so easy and kids just love it!

Makes 8 servings

8 oz. ground beef
2 cans ranch style beans, 15 oz. size
2 cans condensed minestrone soup, 10.75 oz. size
2 cans diced tomatoes with green chiles, 10 oz. size

In a dutch oven over medium heat, add the ground beef. Stir frequently to break the ground beef into crumbles as it cooks. Cook for 8 minutes or until the ground beef is well browned and no longer pink. Drain off the excess grease.

Add the ranch beans with sauce, minestrone soup and tomatoes with juice to the pan. Stir until combined and bring to a boil. Reduce the heat to medium low. Simmer for 15 minutes. Remove the pan from the heat and serve.

Stuffed Pepper Soup

Makes 6 servings

8 oz. pouch Uncle Ben's ready to serve long grain & wild rice
1 lb. ground beef
2 cups frozen chopped green bell peppers, thawed
1 cup chopped onion
26 oz. jar tomato pasta sauce
14 oz. can diced Italian tomatoes
14 oz. can beef broth

Microwave the rice according to the package directions. Let the rice cool while you prepare the rest of the dish. In a dutch oven over medium heat, add the ground beef, green bell peppers and onion. Stir frequently to break the ground beef into crumbles as it cooks. Cook for 8 minutes or until the ground beef is well browned and no longer pink. Drain off the excess grease.

Add the rice, pasta sauce, tomatoes with juice and beef broth to the pan. Stir until combined and bring to a boil. Simmer for 2 minutes. Remove the pan from the heat and serve.

Vegetable Beef Soup

Makes 3 1/2 quarts

4 cups cubed peeled potatoes
6 cups water
1 lb. ground beef
5 tsp. beef bouillon granules
10.75 oz. can condensed tomato soup
2 cups frozen whole kernel corn, thawed
2 cups frozen cut green beans, thawed
2 cups frozen sliced okra, thawed
3 tbs. dried minced onion

In a dutch oven over medium heat, add the potatoes and water. Bring to a boil and reduce the heat to medium low. Place a lid on the pan. Cook for 10 minutes or until the potatoes are tender.

While the potatoes are cooking, add the ground beef to a skillet over medium heat. Stir frequently to break the ground beef into crumbles as it cooks. Cook for 8 minutes or until the ground beef is well browned and no longer pink. Remove the skillet from the heat and drain off the excess grease.

Add the ground beef to the potatoes. Add the beef bouillon granules, tomato soup, corn, green beans, okra and onion. Stir until combined. Stir occasionally and simmer for 10-12 minutes or until the vegetables are tender. Remove the pan from the heat and serve.

Beef Cabbage Soup

Makes 9 servings

1 tbs. vegetable oil
2 lb. beef chuck roast
2 quarts water
8 cups chopped cabbage
1 cup chopped onion
1 cup thinly sliced carrots
2 tbs. granulated sugar
1/2 tsp. paprika
1/4 tsp. Tabasco sauce
15 oz. can sauerkraut, rinsed & drained
15 oz. can diced tomatoes
6 oz. can tomato paste

In a large dutch oven over medium heat, add the vegetable oil. When the oil is hot, add the roast. Brown for 3 minutes on all sides. Add the water to the pan. Bring to a boil and reduce the heat to medium low. Place a lid on the pan. Simmer for 2 to 2 1/2 hours or until the roast is tender. Remove the pan from the heat.

Remove the roast from the pan and cool for 10 minutes. Cut the roast into bite size pieces. Cool the broth for 20 minutes and skim the fat from the broth. Place the pan back on the stove over medium heat. Add the cabbage, onion, carrots, granulated sugar, paprika, Tabasco sauce, sauerkraut, tomatoes with juice and tomato paste to the pan. Stir until combined.

Bring the soup to a boil and reduce the heat to medium low. Place a lid on the pan. Stir occasionally and simmer for 50 minutes. Add the roast to the soup. Stir until combined and cook for 10 minutes. Remove the pan from the heat and serve.

Hamburger Vegetable Soup

Makes about 1 gallon

1 lb. ground beef
1 cup chopped onion
1/2 cup chopped green bell pepper
4 garlic cloves, minced
8 cups beef broth
2 cans Italian stewed tomatoes, 14 oz. size
10 oz. pkg. frozen cut green beans
1 cup ditalini pasta or elbow macaroni
1 tbs. Worcestershire sauce
2 tsp. dried oregano
1 tsp. dried basil
1/2 tsp. black pepper

In a large dutch oven over medium heat, add the ground beef, onion, green bell pepper and garlic. Stir frequently to break the ground beef into crumbles as it cooks. Cook for 8 minutes or until the ground beef is no longer pink and browned. Drain off the excess grease.

Add the beef broth, tomatoes with juice, green beans, macaroni, Worcestershire sauce, oregano, basil and black pepper to the pan. Stir until combined and bring to a boil. Reduce the heat to medium low and place a lid on the pan. Stir occasionally and simmer for 30 minutes or until the vegetables and macaroni are tender. Remove the pan from the heat and serve.

Meatball Stew

Makes 2 1/2 quarts

3 beaten eggs
2/3 cup seasoned breadcrumbs
1/3 cup grated Parmesan cheese
1/8 tsp. black pepper
8 oz. ground beef
8 oz. ground veal
8 oz. ground pork
4 potatoes, peeled & cut into small chunks
3 carrots, sliced
1 1/2 cups chopped celery
1 onion, peeled & cut into wedges
1 garlic clove, minced
1 envelope dry onion soup mix
2 1/4 cups water
1 cup frozen green peas, thawed
4 1/2 tsp. minced fresh parsley

In a large mixing bowl, add the eggs, breadcrumbs, Parmesan cheese, black pepper, ground beef, veal and pork. Using your hands, mix until combined. Form the meat into 1 1/2" meatballs.

Preheat the oven to 350°. Line a large baking sheet with aluminum foil. Place the meatballs on the baking sheet. Bake for 20 minutes or until the meatballs are browned and no longer pink. Remove the meatballs from the oven and drain on paper towels.

In a dutch oven over medium heat, add the meatballs, potatoes, carrots, celery, onion and garlic. In a small bowl, add the onion soup mix and water. Whisk until combined and add to the pan. Stir until well combined. Bring to a boil and reduce the heat to medium low. Place a lid on the pan.

Stir occasionally and simmer for 20 minutes. Add the green peas and parsley to the pan. Stir until combined. Cook for 5 minutes or until the vegetables are tender. Remove the pan from the heat and serve.

This stew is hearty but I serve it with meatless vegetable sandwiches.

Beef Barley Soup

Makes 8 servings

2 lbs. beef stew meat, cut into 1" pieces
1 tbs. vegetable oil
5 cups water
4 celery ribs, chopped
4 carrots, chopped
1 1/4 cups chopped onion
14 oz. can diced tomatoes
2 tbs. tomato paste
4 tsp. beef bouillon granules
1 tsp. dried oregano
1 tsp. dried thyme
1 tsp. dried basil
1 tsp. dried parsley flakes
1/2 tsp. salt
1/4 tsp. black pepper
1 cup quick cooking barley

In a dutch oven over medium heat, add the beef stew meat and vegetable oil. Cook for 10 minutes or until the meat is well browned. Drain off the excess grease.

Add the water, celery, carrots, onion, tomatoes with juice, tomato paste, beef bouillon granules, oregano, thyme, basil, parsley flakes, salt and black pepper to the pan. Stir until combined and bring to a boil. Reduce the heat to medium low and place a lid on the pan.

Simmer for 50 minutes or until the beef and vegetables are tender. Add the barley to the pan. Stir until combined. Place a lid on the pan and simmer for 10 minutes or until the barley is tender. Remove the pan from the heat and serve.

In A Hurry Beef Stew

Keep the ingredients on hand for a hearty meal that taste like homemade!

Makes 6 servings

24 oz. can beef stew
14 oz. can diced stewed tomatoes
10.75 oz. can condensed vegetable beef soup
1 cup cooked whole kernel corn
1/8 tsp. Tabasco sauce

Add all the ingredients to a sauce pan over medium heat. Stir constantly and cook about 5 minutes or until the soup is boiling. Remove the pan from the heat and serve.

Meaty Black Bean Chili

Makes 10 cups

1 lb. ground beef
1 1/2 cups chopped onion
3 garlic cloves, minced
3 cans black beans, 15 oz. size
4 tsp. chili powder
1 tsp. ground cumin
1/2 tsp. black pepper
1/4 tsp. salt
2 cans petite diced tomatoes with jalapenos, 14 oz. size
2 cups water
1 vegetable bouillon cube

In a dutch oven over medium heat, add the ground beef, onion and garlic. Stir frequently to break the ground beef into crumbles as it cooks. Cook for 8 minutes or until the ground beef is well browned and no longer pink. Drain off the excess grease.

Rinse and drain 2 cans black beans. Do not drain the third can. Add the chili powder, cumin, black pepper and salt to the pan. Stir until combined and cook for 2 minutes.

Add the tomatoes with juice, black beans, water and vegetable bouillon cube to the pan. Stir until combined and bring to a boil. Reduce the heat to low. Stir occasionally and simmer for 30 minutes. Remove from the heat and serve.

Beef Noodle Soup

Makes 8 servings

1 lb. ground beef
46 oz. can V-8 juice
1 envelope dry onion soup mix
3 oz. pkg. beef ramen noodles
16 oz. pkg. frozen mixed vegetables

In a large sauce pan over medium heat, add the ground beef. Stir frequently to break the ground beef into crumbles as it cooks. Cook for 8 minutes or until the ground beef is well browned and no longer pink. Drain off the excess grease.

Add the V-8 juice, onion soup mix, seasoning packet from the noodles and mixed vegetables to the pan. Stir until combined and bring to a boil. Reduce the heat to medium low. Simmer for 10 minutes or until the vegetables are tender. Add the noodles to the pan. Stir until combined and cook for 3 minutes or until the noodles are tender. Remove the pan from the heat and serve.

Cheesy Mac Chili

Makes 4 servings

1 lb. ground beef
1/2 cup chopped onion
15 oz. can tomato sauce
3/4 cup water
1/2 cup finely chopped celery
1/2 cup dry elbow macaroni
2 tsp. chili powder
1/2 tsp. salt
15 oz. can red kidney beans, rinsed & drained
4 oz. American cheese, sliced

In a large sauce pan over medium heat, add the ground beef and onion. Stir frequently to break the ground beef into crumbles as it cooks. Cook for 8 minutes or until the ground beef is well browned and no longer pink. Drain off the excess grease.

Add the tomato sauce, water, celery, macaroni, chili powder and salt to the pan. Stir until combined and bring to a boil. Reduce the heat to low and place a lid on the pan. Simmer for 20 minutes or until the macaroni is tender. Add the kidney beans and American cheese to the pan. Stir until combined and the cheese melts. Simmer for 2 minutes. Remove the pan from the heat and serve.

Mexican Vegetable Soup

Makes 10 servings

1 lb. ground beef
1 envelope taco seasoning mix
6 cups tomato juice
15 oz. can chili hot beans
1 lb. pkg. frozen mixed vegetables
12 oz. can tomato paste
2 cups shredded cheddar cheese

In a dutch oven over medium heat, add the ground beef. Stir frequently to break the ground beef into crumbles as it cooks. Cook for 8 minutes or until the ground beef is well browned and no longer pink. Drain off the excess grease.

Add the taco seasoning mix, tomato juice, chili beans with sauce, mixed vegetables and tomato paste. Stir until combined and bring to a boil. Reduce the heat to low. Stir occasionally and simmer for 20 minutes or until the vegetables are tender. Remove the pan from the heat. Spoon the soup into bowls and sprinkle the cheddar cheese over the top.

Homemade Beef Vegetable Soup

Makes 10 cups

1 lb. meaty beef shank bone
2 1/2 quarts plus 1 1/2 tbs. water
15 oz. can stewed tomatoes, undrained & chopped
1 1/2 cups frozen lima beans
1 cup fresh corn kernels
1/2 cup chopped onion
1 large potato, peeled & cubed
1 large carrot, sliced
1 tsp. salt
1 tsp. dried Italian seasoning
1/2 tsp. black pepper
1/2 tsp. Tabasco sauce
1 bay leaf
1 1/2 tbs. all purpose flour

In a dutch oven over medium heat, add the beef bone and 2 1/2 quarts water. Bring to a boil and reduce the heat to low. Place a lid on the pan and simmer for 1 hour. Remove the pan from the heat and refrigerate for 8 hours.

Remove the fat from the top of the broth. Remove the bone and remove any meat from the bone. Strain the broth and add back to the pan. Add the removed meat to the pan. Place the broth on the stove over medium heat and bring to a boil.

Add the tomatoes, lima beans, corn, onion, potato, carrot, salt, Italian seasoning, black pepper, Tabasco sauce and bay leaf. Stir until combined and bring to a boil. Reduce the heat to medium low and place a lid on the pan. Stir occasionally and simmer for 1 hour or until the vegetables are tender. Remove the bay leaf from the pan and discard.

In a small bowl, add 1 1/2 tablespoons water and the all purpose flour. Whisk until combined and add to the soup. Stir constantly and cook for 3 minutes or until the soup thickens. Remove the pan from the heat and serve.

2 CHICKEN & TURKEY SOUPS & SANDWICHES

Chicken sandwiches have grown in popularity over the years but chicken soup has always been a classic comfort food.

Baked Turkey Southwest Sandwiches

Makes 8 servings

1 cup sliced black olives
1/2 tsp. chili powder
1/2 tsp. ground cumin
1/4 tsp. salt
1/2 cup mayonnaise
1/3 cup sour cream
1/2 cup sliced green onions
8 slices Italian bread, about 1/2" thick
1 lb. thinly sliced deli turkey
2 tomatoes, thinly sliced
2 avocados, peeled and sliced
1 cup shredded cheddar cheese
1 cup shredded Pepper Jack cheese

Preheat the oven to 350°. In a mixing bowl, add the black olives, chili powder, cumin, salt, mayonnaise, sour cream and green onions. Stir until combined and spread on one side of each bread slice. Place the bread slices, topping side up, on a baking sheet.

Place the turkey over the bread slices. Place the tomatoes and avocados over the turkey. Sprinkle the cheddar cheese and Pepper Jack cheese over the top of the sandwiches. Bake for 15 minutes or until the sandwiches are toasted, hot and the cheeses melted. Remove the sandwiches from the oven and serve.

Turkey Pancetta Sandwiches

Makes 6 sandwiches

12 slices sourdough bread
5 oz. ripened blue cheese spread
1 1/2 lbs. roasted turkey, sliced
1/2 cup whole berry cranberry sauce
12 pancetta slices, cooked
2 cups arugula
1/4 cup stone grain mustard

Spread one side of 6 sourdough bread slices with the blue cheese. Place the turkey over the blue cheese. Spoon the cranberry sauce over the turkey. Place the pancetta over the top. Place the arugula over the top of the sandwiches.

Spread one side of remaining 6 bread slices with the mustard. Place the bread on the sandwiches with the mustard side down and serve.

Smoked Turkey Monte Cristo Sandwiches

Makes 4 servings

4 tbs. whole grain mustard
8 bread slices
8 oz. smoked turkey, thinly sliced
4 slices Swiss cheese, 1 oz. size
2 eggs
1/3 cup whole milk
2 tbs. unsalted butter
2 tbs. blackberry preserves
Powdered sugar for dusting, optional

Spread the mustard on one side of each bread slice. Place the turkey and Swiss cheese over the mustard on 4 bread slices. Place the remaining bread slices, mustard side down, over the sandwiches.

In a shallow dish, add the eggs and milk. Whisk until well combined. Dip both sides of the sandwiches in the egg wash. In a skillet over medium heat, add the butter. When the butter melts, add the sandwiches. Cook for 3-4 minutes on each side or until golden brown. Remove the skillet from the heat. Place the sandwiches on a platter. Spread the blackberry preserves over the top of the sandwiches. Sprinkle powdered sugar to taste over the top and serve.

Waldorf Turkey Sandwiches

Makes 4 servings

1 1/4 cups cubed cooked turkey breast
1 cup chopped apple
1/4 cup diced celery
3 tbs. mayonnaise
2 tbs. plain yogurt
2 tbs. chopped walnuts
1 tbs. raisins
1/8 tsp. ground nutmeg
1/8 tsp. ground cinnamon
8 raisin bread slices, toasted
4 lettuce leaves

In a mixing bowl, add the turkey breast, apple, celery, mayonnaise, yogurt, walnuts, raisins, nutmeg and cinnamon. Stir until well combined. Cover the bowl and refrigerate for 1 hour.

Remove the filling from the refrigerator and spread about 3/4 cup filling on one side of 4 bread slices. Place the lettuce leaves over the filling. Place the remaining bread slices over the top and serve.

Cheesy Garlic Chicken Sandwiches

Makes 4 servings

1 lb. boneless skinless chicken breast, cut into thin strips
1 envelope dry Caesar salad dressing mix
2 tbs. olive oil
1 cup sliced fresh mushrooms
1/2 cup sliced purple onion
4 slices frozen Texas Toast garlic bread
4 slices provolone cheese

Add the chicken to a mixing bowl. Sprinkle the Caesar dressing mix over the chicken. Toss until the chicken is coated in the seasoning. In a skillet over medium heat, add the olive oil. When the oil is hot, add the mushrooms and purple onion. Saute for 5 minutes. Remove the vegetables from the skillet and set aside.

Add the chicken to the skillet. Cook for 6 minutes or until the chicken is no longer pink and tender. Remove the skillet from the heat. Preheat the oven to 350°. Place the garlic bread slices on a baking pan. Bake for 3 minutes.

Spoon the chicken and vegetables over the top of the garlic bread. Place a provolone cheese slice over each sandwich. Bake for 5 minutes or until the garlic bread is toasted and the cheese melted. Remove the sandwiches from the oven and serve.

Grilled Barbecue Chicken Sandwiches

Makes 4 sandwiches

4 boneless skinless chicken breast, 6 oz. size
1 tbs. beer can chicken seasoning
1/3 cup bottled hickory smoked barbecue sauce
4 slices provolone cheese, 1 oz. size
4 hamburger buns, split and toasted
1 cup prepared coleslaw

Place the chicken breast between 2 sheets of plastic wrap. Pound the chicken with a meat mallet until about 1/2" thick. Remove the plastic wrap and sprinkle the beer can chicken seasoning over the chicken.

Have your grill hot and ready. Place the chicken on the grill over medium coals or 350°. Cook for 3-4 minutes on each side or until the chicken is no longer pink. Brush the barbecue sauce over the chicken and remove the chicken from the grill. Let the chicken rest for 5 minutes.

Place one provolone cheese slice on the bottom of each bun. Place a chicken breast on each sandwich. Spoon the coleslaw over the chicken. Place the top on the sandwiches and serve.

Open Face Buffalo Chicken Sandwiches

Makes 6 sandwiches

6 frozen Texas Toast garlic bread slices
4 cups cooked shredded chicken
1/4 tsp. garlic powder
1/8 tsp. salt
1/8 tsp. black pepper
1/4 cup Tabasco sauce
1/4 cup unsalted butter
1 tbs. honey
2 cups thinly sliced cucumbers
1/2 cup prepared ranch dressing

Preheat the oven to 450°. Place the garlic bread slices on a baking pan. Bake for 5-7 minutes or until the garlic bread is toasted and golden brown. Remove the bread from the oven.

While the garlic bread is baking, add the chicken, garlic powder, salt, black pepper, Tabasco sauce, butter and honey to a skillet over medium heat. Stir constantly and cook for 5 minutes or until the butter melts and the chicken is hot. Remove the skillet from the heat.

Place the garlic bread slices on a serving platter. Spoon the chicken over the garlic bread. Place the cucumber slices over the chicken. Drizzle the ranch dressing over the top and serve.

Chicken Cheddar Wraps

Makes 12 wraps

1 cup sour cream
1 cup chunky salsa
2 tbs. mayonnaise
4 cups cubed cooked chicken
2 cups shredded cheddar cheese
1 cup thinly sliced fresh mushrooms
1 cup guacamole
12 flour tortillas, 6" size
2 cups shredded lettuce

In a mixing bowl, add the sour cream, salsa and mayonnaise. Stir until combined. Add the chicken, cheddar cheese and mushrooms to the bowl. Stir until combined.

Spread the guacamole on one side of each tortilla. Spoon the chicken salad over the guacamole. Sprinkle the lettuce over the top. Roll up and serve.

Buffalo Chicken Wraps

Makes 4 servings

1 cup all purpose flour
1 tsp. salt
1/4 tsp. black pepper
1/2 cup buttermilk
1 cup vegetable oil
4 boneless skinless chicken breast, 4 oz. size
1/4 cup melted unsalted butter
4 spinach tortillas, 10" size
1 cup shredded lettuce
1 cup shredded cheddar cheese
2/3 cup chopped tomatoes
1/2 cup blue cheese salad dressing

In a shallow dish, add the all purpose flour, salt and black pepper. Whisk until combined. In a shallow bowl, add the buttermilk. In a deep skillet over medium high heat, add the vegetable oil. When the oil is hot, dip each chicken breast in the buttermilk and dredge each chicken breast in the flour. Place the chicken in the hot oil.

Cook about 4-5 minutes on each side or until the chicken is golden brown and no longer pink. Remove the chicken from the oil and drain on paper towels. Let the chicken rest for 5 minutes. Cut the chicken into thin strips.

In a mixing bowl, add the Tabasco sauce and butter. Whisk until combined and add the chicken. Toss until the chicken strips are coated in the sauce. Place the chicken strips in the center of the tortillas. Sprinkle the lettuce, cheddar cheese and tomatoes over the chicken. Drizzle the dressing over the top. Roll the wraps up and serve.

Pepper Chicken Pita Wraps

Makes 6 servings

6 boneless skinless chicken breast, 5 oz. size
1/4 cup teriyaki sauce
1 tsp. dried thyme
1 tsp. ground white pepper
1 tsp. black pepper
1/2 tsp. garlic powder
1/2 tsp. cayenne pepper
2 tbs. olive oil
6 pita bread rounds, 8" size
2/3 cup mayonnaise
2 tbs. prepared horseradish
3 cups shredded lettuce

Cut the chicken breast into 1/2" strips and place in a shallow dish. Pour the teriyaki sauce over the chicken. Toss until the chicken strips are coated in the sauce. Cover the dish and refrigerate for 2 hours.

Remove the chicken from the refrigerator and drain off the marinade. Sprinkle the thyme, white pepper, black pepper, garlic powder and cayenne pepper over the chicken. Toss until the chicken is coated in the seasonings.

In a large skillet over medium heat, add the olive oil. When the oil is hot, add the chicken. Saute for 5 minutes or until the chicken is no longer pink and well browned. Remove the skillet from the heat.

Wrap the pita rounds in plastic wrap. Microwave for 30 seconds or until they are warm and flexible. In a small bowl, add the mayonnaise and horseradish. Stir until combined and spread on the inside of the pita breads. Sprinkle the lettuce over the mayonnaise. Spoon the chicken into the pitas. Fold the pitas over and serve.

Salsa Ranch Chicken Wraps

Makes 4 servings

4 tbs. salsa
4 tbs. ranch salad dressing
4 tomato basil tortillas, 10" size
2 grilled boneless skinless chicken breast, cut into thin strips
12 cucumber slices
8 tomato slices
1/2 cup green bell pepper, julienned
6 slices Swiss cheese, 1 oz. size
2 tbs. unsalted butter

Spread the salsa and ranch dressing over one side of each tortilla. Place the chicken, cucumber, tomato and green bell pepper in the center of each tortilla. Place 1 1/2 cheese slices over the filling in each tortilla. Roll the sandwiches up.

In a large skillet over medium heat, add the butter. When the butter melts, add the wraps. Cook for 3 minutes on each side or until the cheese melts and the wraps are golden brown. Remove the skillet from the heat and serve.

Guacamole Chicken Wraps

Makes 4 servings

1/2 cup guacamole
4 spinach tortillas, 8" size
1 cup shredded Mexican cheese blend
12 oz. cooked boneless skinless chicken breast
1 tsp. ground cumin
1 tsp. chili powder
4 lettuce leaves

Spread the guacamole on one side of each tortilla. Sprinkle the Mexican cheese blend over guacamole. Cut the chicken breast into thin strips and place in a skillet over medium heat. Sprinkle the cumin and chili powder over the chicken. Stir constantly and cook for 3 minutes or until the chicken is hot. Remove the skillet from the heat.

Place a lettuce leaf on each tortilla. Spoon the chicken over the lettuce. Tightly roll up and serve.

Chicken Spinach Panini

Makes 4 servings

6 oz. pkg. baby fresh spinach
2 tsp. olive oil
1/4 cup unsalted butter, softened
8 slices sourdough bread
1/4 cup bottled creamy Italian salad dressing
8 slices provolone cheese, 1 oz. size
8 oz. thinly sliced cooked chicken breast
2 slices purple onion, separated into rings

In a large skillet over medium heat, add the spinach and olive oil. Saute for 3 minutes or until the spinach wilts. Remove the skillet from the heat. Spread the butter on one side of each bread slice.

Spread the Italian dressing on the unbuttered sides of 4 bread slices. Place 1 provolone cheese slice over the dressing on each sandwich. Place the chicken, spinach and onions over the cheese. Place the remaining cheese slices over the sandwiches. Place the remaining bread, butter side up, over the sandwiches.

Place the sandwiches on a hot panini press and cook for 3 minutes or until golden brown. To cook the sandwiches in a skillet, place a large skillet over medium heat. Add the sandwiches to the skillet. Cook about 3 minutes on each side or until the cheese melts and the sandwiches are golden brown. Remove the skillet from the heat and serve.

Jerked Chicken Sandwiches

Makes 4 sandwiches

3 tbs. Caribbean Jerk seasoning
3 lbs. boneless skinless chicken thighs
1 red bell pepper, chopped
1 1/2 cups chopped onion
1/2 cup chicken broth
1/4 cup ketchup
4 hoagie buns, split and toasted

Rub the Caribbean Jerk seasoning over the chicken thighs. Place the thighs in a 5 quart slow cooker. Add the red bell pepper, onion, chicken broth and ketchup to the slow cooker. Stir until combined.

Set the temperature to low. Cook for 6 hours or until the chicken is no longer pink and tender. Shred the chicken using two forks. Stir until combined. Using a slotted spoon, spoon the chicken onto the bottom hoagie buns. Place the top on the buns and serve.

Turkey Guacamole Subs

Makes 4 servings

1 avocado, peeled and mashed
1 tbs. lemon juice
1 tbs. mayonnaise
1/4 tsp. Tabasco sauce
1 garlic clove, minced
16 oz. loaf Italian bread
8 oz. cooked turkey, cut into 1" slices
1 large tomato, sliced
1/4 cup chopped green onions
8 oz. pkg. sliced Pepper Jack cheese
12 black olives, sliced

In a mixing bowl, add the avocado, lemon juice, mayonnaise, Tabasco sauce and garlic. Stir until well combined. Cut the bread in half crosswise. Slice each piece in half horizontally. Place the bread slices on a baking sheet. Turn the oven to the broiler position. Broil about 2 minutes on each side or until the bread is lightly toasted. Remove the bread from the oven but leave the oven on.

Spread the avocado mixture on one side of each bread slice. Top each bread slice with the turkey and tomato. Sprinkle the green onions over the sandwiches. Place the Pepper Jack cheese slices over the sandwiches. Sprinkle the black olives over the top. Place the sandwiches on a baking sheet. Broil the sandwiches for 2 minutes or until the cheese melts. Remove the sandwiches from the oven and serve.

Cherry Chicken Salad Croissants

Makes 7 servings

2 1/2 cups cubed cooked chicken breast
2/3 cup dried cherries
1/3 cup chopped celery
1/3 cup chopped apple
1/3 cup toasted pecans, chopped
1/2 cup mayonnaise
4 tsp. whole milk
1/2 tsp. salt
1/8 tsp. black pepper
7 croissants, split and toasted

In a mixing bowl, add the chicken, cherries, celery, apple and pecans. In a small bowl, add the mayonnaise, milk, salt and black pepper. Stir until combined and add to the salad. Stir until combined. Spoon the chicken salad on the bottom of the croissants. Place the top on the croissants and serve.

Open Face Turkey Hero Sandwiches

Makes 12 servings

3 cups thinly sliced fresh mushrooms
1 cup Italian salad dressing
16 oz. loaf unsliced French bread
2 cups chopped lettuce
1 1/2 lbs. thinly sliced smoked turkey
2 large tomatoes, thinly sliced
2 cups shredded mozzarella cheese

In a mixing bowl, add the mushrooms and 1 cup Italian salad dressing. Toss until the mushrooms are coated in the salad dressing. Cover the bowl and chill for 1 hour. Remove the mushrooms from the refrigerator and drain all the dressing from the mushrooms.

Cut the bread in half lengthwise. Scoop out the inside of the loaf leaving about a 1/2" shell on the loaf. Spoon the mushrooms into the bread halves. Place the lettuce over the mushrooms. Place the turkey slices over the lettuce. Place the tomatoes over the turkey. Place the bread halves on a baking sheet. Sprinkle the mozzarella cheese over the top of the sandwiches.

Turn the oven to the broiler position. Broil the sandwiches for 5 minutes. Remove the sandwiches from the oven and cut into slices to serve.

Creamy Turkey Melt

Makes 4 servings

1/2 cup chopped purple onion
5 tbs. softened unsalted butter
3 oz. cream cheese, cubed
1/3 cup sour cream
2 cups cubed cooked turkey
8 slices sandwich bread
4 slices Swiss cheese

In a skillet over medium heat, add the onion and 1 tablespoon butter. Saute for 4 minutes or until the onion is tender. Add the cream cheese and sour cream to the skillet. Stir until the cream cheese melts. Add the turkey and cook only until the turkey is heated. Remove the skillet from the heat.

Spread the turkey on 4 bread slices. Place a Swiss cheese slice over the filling. Place the remaining bread slices over the top. Spread the remaining butter on the outside bread slices of each sandwich.

In a skillet over medium heat, add the sandwiches. Cook for 3 minutes on each side or until the sandwiches are golden brown. Remove the skillet from the heat and serve.

Mexican Tomato Chicken Soup

Makes 4 servings

6 corn tortillas, 6" size
2 tbs. vegetable oil
Salt and black pepper to taste
2 fresh tomatoes, cored and halved
1 cup chopped onion
2 garlic cloves, minced
4 cups chicken broth
2 cups tomato juice
1 bay leaf
1/4 tsp. ground cumin
1/4 tsp. ground coriander
1/4 tsp. cayenne pepper
1 lb. boneless skinless chicken breast, cut into 1/2" strips
4 green onions, thinly sliced
1/2 cup fresh lime juice
1/4 cup chopped fresh cilantro
1/2 cup crumbled queso fresco
1 avocado, peeled, pitted & chopped

Brush one side of each corn tortilla with 1 tablespoon vegetable oil. Cut the tortillas in half. Stack the tortillas on top of each other. Cut into 1/4" strips. Preheat the oven to 400°. Spread the tortilla strips on a large baking pan. Sprinkle with salt and black pepper to taste. Stir occasionally and bake for 15 minutes or until golden brown. Remove from the oven and set aside.

In a skillet over high heat, add the tomatoes. Cook for 2 minutes on each side or until the tomatoes are charred. Remove the tomatoes from the skillet and add to a food processor. Add the onion and 1 tablespoon vegetable oil to the skillet. Saute for 3 minutes. Add the garlic to the skillet. Saute for 2 minutes. Remove the skillet from the heat and add the onion and garlic to the food processor. Process until smooth.

In a dutch oven over medium heat, add the tomato puree. Stir constantly and cook for 5 minutes. Add the chicken broth, tomato juice, bay leaf, cumin, coriander and cayenne pepper to the pan. Stir until combined and bring to a boil. Reduce the heat to low. Stir occasionally and simmer for 20 minutes.

Add the chicken to the pan. Cook for 7 minutes or until the chicken is tender and no longer pink. Remove the pan from the heat. Remove the bay leaf and discard. Add the green onions, lime juice and cilantro to the pan. Stir until combined.

Spoon the soup into bowls. Sprinkle the tortilla strips, queso fresco and avocado over the top and serve.

Delicious with most any sandwich especially grilled cheeses or meatless sandwiches.

Chicken Alphabet Soup

Why buy the canned chicken soup when you can make a homemade version in no time?

Makes 10 servings

3 carrots, chopped
2 celery ribs, chopped
3/4 cup chopped onion
1 tbs. olive oil
8 cups chicken broth
3 cups cubed cooked chicken
1/4 tsp. dried thyme
1 1/2 cups alphabet pasta
3 tbs. minced fresh parsley

In a large sauce pan over medium heat, add the carrots, celery, onion and olive oil. Saute for 6 minutes or until the vegetables are tender. Add the chicken broth, chicken and alphabet pasta to the pan. Stir until combined. Bring the soup to a boil and reduce the heat to medium low. Simmer for 10 minutes or until the pasta is tender. Remove the pan from the heat and stir in the parsley.

Chicken Rice Tortilla Soup

Makes 5 servings

10.75 oz. can condensed chicken rice soup
1 1/3 cups water
1 cup salsa
1 cup canned pinto beans, rinsed & drained
1 cup canned black beans, rinsed & drained
1 cup frozen whole kernel corn
1 cup cooked diced chicken
1 tsp. ground cumin
1 cup crushed tortilla chips
1/2 cup shredded cheddar cheese
1/3 cup sour cream

In a sauce pan over medium heat, add the chicken rice soup, water, salsa, pinto beans, black beans, corn, chicken and cumin. Stir until combined and bring to a boil. Cook for 8 minutes or until the corn is tender. Remove the pan from the heat. Spoon into bowls. Sprinkle the tortilla chips and cheddar cheese over the soup. Spoon a dollop of sour cream over the top and serve.

Homemade Chicken Rice Soup

Makes 10 servings

3 lbs. meaty chicken pieces
10 cups water
1/2 cup chopped onion
2 1/2 tsp. salt
1/2 tsp. dried thyme
1/4 tsp. black pepper
1 cup thinly sliced celery
1 cup thinly sliced carrots
1/2 cup long grain rice

In a stock pot over medium heat, add the chicken and water. Bring the chicken to a boil and skim off any foam that rises to the surface. Reduce the heat to medium low and place a lid on the pan. Simmer for 15 minutes.

Add the onion, salt, thyme and black pepper to the pan. Place the lid back on the pan and simmer for 40 minutes or until the chicken is no longer pink and tender. Remove the pan from the heat.

Remove the chicken from the pot and cool for 20 minutes. Cool the broth for 20 minutes and skim off the fat. Remove the meat from the chicken and cut into bite size pieces. Add the chicken back to the broth.

Place the pan back on the stove over medium heat. When the broth is boiling, stir in the celery, carrots and rice. Place a lid on the pan and simmer for 20 minutes or until the vegetables and rice are tender. Remove the pan from the heat and serve.

Slow Cooker Chicken Stew

Makes 6 servings

1 1/2 cups all purpose flour
1 1/2 tsp. salt
1/2 tsp. white pepper
3 lbs. meaty chicken pieces, skin removed
2 tbs. vegetable oil
3 cups chicken broth
6 large carrots, cut into 1" pieces
2 celery ribs, cut into 1/2" pieces
1 large onion, thinly sliced
1 1/2 tsp. crushed dried rosemary
1 1/2 cups frozen green peas
2 tsp. baking powder
1 beaten egg
1/2 cup whole milk

In a Ziploc bag, add 1/2 cup all purpose flour, 1 teaspoon salt and white pepper. Close the bag and shake until combined. Add the chicken pieces to the bag. Close the bag and shake until the chicken is coated in the seasoned flour.

In a large skillet over medium heat, add the vegetable oil. When the oil is hot, add the chicken. Cook for 4 minutes on each side or until browned. Remove the chicken from the skillet and drain on paper towels.

Add the chicken broth to the skillet. Stir constantly and bring the broth to a boil. Remove the skillet from the heat. Place the carrots, celery and onion in a 5 quart slow cooker. Sprinkle 1 teaspoon rosemary over the vegetables. Place the chicken over the vegetables. Pour the hot broth over the chicken.

Set the temperature to low. Cook for 6-7 hours or until the chicken is no longer pink and the chicken and vegetables are tender. Add the green peas to the slow cooker. Stir until combined.

In a mixing bowl, add 1 cup all purpose flour, baking powder, 1/2 teaspoon salt, 1/2 teaspoon rosemary, egg and milk. Stir until combined. The stew must be bubbly before adding the dumplings. Drop the dumplings, by tablespoonfuls, over the stew.

Increase the temperature to high. Cook for 25-30 minutes or until a toothpick inserted in the dumplings comes out clean. Do not lift the lid while the dumplings are cooking.

Chicken Broccoli Stew With Lemon Dumplings

Makes 6 servings

3 lbs. meaty chicken pieces
4 cups water
1/2 cup chopped onion
1 1/4 tsp. salt
1/4 tsp. black pepper
1/4 tsp. dried tarragon
1/2 cup cold water
1 1/4 cups all purpose flour
1 tbs. finely chopped parsley
1 tsp. baking powder
1/2 tsp. grated lemon zest
1/4 cup whole milk
1 tbs. vegetable oil
1 tsp. lemon juice
1 beaten egg
10 oz. pkg. frozen cut broccoli

In a large dutch oven over medium heat, add the chicken and 4 cups water. Bring to a boil and skim off the foam that rises to the surface. Add the onion, 1 teaspoon salt, black pepper and tarragon to the pan. Reduce the heat to low and place a lid on the pan.

Simmer for 45 minutes or until the chicken is tender. Remove the pan from the heat. Remove the chicken from the pan and cool for 20 minutes. Remove the meat from the bones and cut into bite size pieces. Cool the broth for 20 minutes and skim the fat from the broth.

Place the broth back on the stove medium heat. Bring the broth to a boil. In a small bowl, add 1/2 cup cold water and 1/2 cup all purpose flour. Whisk until combined and add to the broth. Stir constantly and cook about 4 minutes or until the broth thickens and bubbles.

In a mixing bowl, add 3/4 cup all purpose flour, parsley, baking powder, lemon zest, 1/4 teaspoon salt, milk, vegetable oil, lemon juice and egg. Stir until moistened and combined.

Add the chicken and broccoli to the pan. Stir until combined and bring the broth back to a boil. Drop the dumplings, by teaspoonfuls, into the broth. Reduce the heat to low.

Place a lid on the pan. Simmer for 6-8 minutes or until the dumplings are tender and fluffy. Remove the pan from the heat and serve.

Oriental Chicken Stew

Makes 4 servings

2 tbs. vegetable oil
1 lb. boneless skinless chicken breast, cut into 1" cubes
1 garlic clove, minced
2 cups water
8 oz. can pineapple tidbits
1/3 cup dry long grain rice
1/4 cup cider vinegar
3 tbs. light brown sugar
2 tbs. soy sauce
1/2 tsp. salt
1/2 tsp. finely chopped fresh ginger
1/8 tsp. black pepper
1/2 cup green bell pepper, cut into 1" pieces
1/2 cup red bell pepper, cut into 1" pieces
3 tbs. cold water
2 tbs. cornstarch

In a large skillet over medium heat, add the vegetable oil. When the oil is hot, add the chicken and garlic. Saute for 4 minutes. Add 2 cups water to the skillet. Drain the pineapple but reserve the juice. Add the pineapple juice, rice, cider vinegar, brown sugar, soy sauce, salt, ginger and black pepper to the skillet. Stir until combined.

Stir occasionally and cook for 12 minutes or until the rice is almost tender. Add the green bell pepper, red bell pepper and pineapple to the skillet. Stir until combined.

In a small bowl, add 3 tablespoons cold water and cornstarch. Whisk until combined and add to the skillet. Stir until combined. Bring the stew to a boil and reduce the heat to low. Place a lid on the skillet. Stir occasionally and simmer for 10 minutes or until the rice and peppers are tender. Remove the skillet from the heat and serve.

Oriental Chicken Noodle Soup

Makes 5 servings

6 cups chicken broth
1 1/2 cups cubed cooked chicken
3/4 tsp. granulated sugar
4 tsp. soy sauce
3/4 cup Chinese noodles, broken into pieces
1 cup sugar snap peas
2 green onions, thinly sliced

In a large sauce pan over medium heat, add the chicken broth, chicken, granulated sugar and soy sauce. Stir until combined and bring to a boil. Add the noodles and sugar snap peas to the pan.

Stir occasionally and simmer for 3-5 minutes or until the noodles and peas are tender. Remove the pan from the heat and spoon into bowls. Sprinkle the green onions over the top and serve.

Country Chicken Soup

Makes 8 servings

2 cups cubed cooked chicken
2 cups frozen mixed vegetables
1/2 cup chopped onion
1 tbs. chopped fresh parsley
1/2 tsp. poultry seasoning
1/2 tsp. dried thyme
9 cups chicken broth
2 cups dry egg noodles

Add all the ingredients to a dutch oven over medium heat. Stir until combined and bring to a boil. Reduce the heat to low. Stir occasionally and simmer for 15 minutes or until the vegetables and pasta are tender. Remove the pan from the heat and serve.

Zesty Chicken Soup

Makes about 1 gallon

4 boneless skinless chicken breast, 6 oz. size
4 cups water
2 onions, chopped
2 celery ribs, chopped
4 garlic cloves, minced
1 tbs. vegetable oil
14 oz. can Mexican diced tomatoes
14 oz. can diced tomatoes
8 oz. can tomato sauce
1 cup salsa
3 zucchini, chopped
2 carrots, sliced
1 cup frozen white corn
4 oz. can chopped green chiles, drained
3 tsp. ground cumin
2 tsp. chili powder
1 tsp. dried basil

In a dutch oven over medium heat, add the chicken breast and water. Bring to a boil and cook for 12 minutes or until the chicken breast are no longer pink. Remove the chicken from the pan and cut into bite size pieces. Add the chicken back to the pan.

In a large skillet over medium heat, add the onions, celery, garlic and vegetable oil. Saute for 10 minutes. Remove from the heat and add the vegetables to the dutch oven.

Add the tomatoes with juice, tomato sauce, salsa, zucchini, carrots, corn, green chiles, cumin, chili powder and basil to the pan. Stir until combined and bring to a boil. Reduce the heat to low and place a lid on the pan. Simmer for 20 minutes or until the vegetables are tender. Remove the pan from the heat and serve.

Chunky Chicken Noodle Soup

Makes 7 cups

3 lb. whole chicken, skin removed
6 cups water
3 fresh celery leaves
1/4 tsp. dried thyme
1/3 cup sliced green onions
1/2 cup sliced celery
1/2 cup sliced carrot
2 tbs. minced fresh parsley
1/2 tsp. salt
1/4 tsp. black pepper
1 tsp. instant chicken bouillon granules
1 cup dry egg noodles
1 bay leaf

In a dutch oven over medium heat, add the chicken, water, celery and thyme. Bring to a boil and reduce the heat to medium low. Place a lid on the pan. Simmer for 1 hour or until the chicken is no longer pink and tender. Remove the pan from the heat.

Remove the chicken from the pan and set aside. Strain the broth and add back to the pan. Remove the chicken from the bones and dice. Add the diced chicken to the pan. Place the pan back on the stove over medium heat. Add the green onions, celery, carrot, parsley, salt, black pepper, chicken bouillon, noodles and bay leaf to the pan. Stir until combined and bring to a boil. Place a lid on the pan and simmer for 20 minutes. Remove the pan from the heat and serve.

Asian Chicken Noodle Soup

Makes 4 servings

4 cups water
2 green onions, chopped
1 tsp. finely chopped fresh ginger
3 oz. pkg. oriental ramen noodles
1 cup sliced bok choy
2 cups chopped cooked chicken

In a sauce pan over medium heat, add the water, green onions and ginger. Bring to a boil and add the noodles to the pan. Boil for 2 minutes. Add the seasoning packet from the noodles along with the bok choy and chicken to the pan. Stir until combined and cook for 2 minutes. Remove the pan from the heat and serve.

Fiesta Chicken Chowder

Makes 2 1/2 quarts

3 tbs. all purpose flour
1 envelope fajita seasoning
1 lb. boneless skinless chicken breast, cubed
3 tbs. vegetable oil
1 cup chopped onion
2 garlic cloves, minced
3 cups water
15 oz. can black beans, rinsed & drained
14 oz. can Mexican stewed tomatoes
11 oz. can Mexicorn, drained
1 cup dry instant brown rice
4 oz. can diced green chiles, drained
11 oz. can condensed nacho cheese soup
3 tbs. minced fresh cilantro
1 tbs. lime juice

In a Ziploc bag, add the all purpose flour and 2 tablespoons fajita seasoning. Whisk until combined. Add the chicken to the bag. Close the bag and shake until the chicken in coated in the seasoned flour.

In a dutch oven over medium heat, add the vegetable oil. When the oil is hot, add the chicken. Saute for 6-8 minutes or until the chicken is well browned, no longer pink and tender. Remove the chicken from the pan and drain on paper towels.

Add the onion and garlic to the pan. Saute for 5 minutes. Add the remaining fajita seasoning, water, black beans, tomatoes with juice, Mexicorn, brown rice and green chiles to the pan. Stir until combined and bring to a boil. Place a lid on the pan and reduce the heat to low. Simmer for 5-7 minutes or until the rice is tender.

Add the nacho cheese soup, cilantro, lime juice and chicken to the pan. Stir until combined and cook only until the soup is thoroughly heated. Remove the pan from the heat and serve.

Western Chicken Chowder

Makes 4 servings

2 tbs. vegetable oil
1 cup chopped onion
1 cup chopped red bell pepper
8 oz. boneless skinless chicken breast, cubed
1 cup chicken broth
1 cup whole milk
15 oz. can sweet potatoes in syrup, rinsed, drained & chopped
10 oz. pkg. frozen whole kernel corn
4 oz. can diced green chiles, drained
1 envelope taco seasoning mix

In a large sauce pan over medium heat, add the vegetable oil. When the oil is hot, add the onion and red bell pepper. Saute for 2 minutes. Add the chicken to the pan. Saute for 3 minutes.

Add the chicken broth, milk, sweet potatoes, corn, green chiles and taco seasoning mix to the pan. Stir until combined and bring to a boil. Reduce the heat to low. Simmer for 10 minutes or until the chicken and corn are tender. Remove the pan from the heat and serve.

Creamy Chicken Vegetable Soup

Another soup that is so easy and delicious!

Makes 4 servings

2 pkgs. frozen broccoli, cauliflower & carrots in cheese sauce, 10 oz. size
2 cups whole milk
2 cups cubed cooked chicken
1 tsp. dried savory
1/2 tsp. black pepper

Add all the ingredients to a sauce pan over medium heat. Stir until combined and bring to a boil. Reduce the heat to low. Stir occasionally and simmer for 10 minutes or until the vegetables are tender. Remove from the heat and serve.

Chicken Gumbo Soup

Makes 8 servings

3 lbs. meaty chicken pieces
6 cups water
1 chicken bouillon cube
1 cup finely chopped onion
3/4 cup chopped green bell pepper
3/4 cup chopped celery
1 tbs. dried parsley flakes
1/2 tsp. cayenne pepper
1/4 tsp. black pepper
28 oz. can diced tomatoes
10 oz. pkg. frozen cut okra
1/4 cup dry long grain rice

In a large dutch oven over medium heat, add the chicken and water. Bring to a boil and skim off any foam that rises to the top. Reduce the heat to medium low. Add the chicken bouillon cube, onion, green bell pepper, celery, parsley flakes, cayenne pepper and black pepper to the pan. Stir until combined.

Place a lid on the pan. Simmer for 45 minutes or until the chicken is no longer pink and tender. Remove the pan from the heat. Remove the chicken from the pan and cool for 20 minutes. Remove the meat from the bones and cut into bite size pieces. Cool the broth for 20 minutes and skim the fat from the broth.

Place the pan back on the stove over medium heat. Add the tomatoes with juice, okra and rice to the pan. Stir until combined and bring to a boil. Reduce the heat to medium low. Place a lid on the pan and simmer for 15 minutes or until the rice is tender. Add the chicken to the pan. Stir until combined and cook for 5 minutes. Remove the pan from the heat and serve.

Chicken Asparagus Soup

Makes 2 quarts

2 lbs. fresh asparagus, trimmed
2 large potatoes, peeled & diced
1 1/4 cups chopped onion
2 celery ribs, chopped
1 carrot, chopped
2 tsp. dried parsley flakes
1 garlic clove, minced
2 tbs. vegetable oil
2 cans chicken broth, 14 oz. size
1 tsp. salt
1/2 tsp. black pepper
1 bay leaf
2 cups cubed cooked chicken
2 cups half and half cream
Shaved Parmesan cheese, optional

Add the asparagus spears to a large skillet over medium heat. Cover the asparagus with water and bring to a boil. Place a lid on the pan and reduce the heat to low. Simmer for 30 minutes. Remove the skillet from the heat. Drain the liquid from the asparagus but save the liquid.

In a dutch oven over medium heat, add the potatoes, onion, celery, carrot, parsley flakes, garlic and vegetable oil. Saute for 12 minutes or until the vegetables are tender. Add the chicken broth, salt, 1/4 teaspoon black pepper and bay leaf to the pan. Bring to a boil and reduce the heat to low. Simmer for 30 minutes. Remove the pan from the heat. Remove the bay leaf and discard. Cool for 15 minutes.

Using a hand blender, puree the soup. Add the chicken, half and half cream, asparagus and 1/4 teaspoon black pepper to the soup. Place the pan back on the stove over medium heat. Cook for 5 minutes or until the soup is thoroughly heated. Do not let the soup boil. Remove the pan from the heat. Spoon into bowls and sprinkle Parmesan cheese over the top if desired.

Chicken Soup With Potato Dumplings

Makes 5 servings

1/4 cup chopped onion
2 garlic cloves, minced
1 tbs. vegetable oil
6 cups chicken broth
2 cups cubed cooked chicken
2 celery ribs, chopped
2 carrots, sliced
1/4 tsp. dried sage
1 1/2 cups Bisquick
1 cup cold mashed potatoes
1/4 cup whole milk
1 tbs. chopped green onion
1/8 tsp. black pepper

In a large sauce pan over medium heat, add the onion, garlic and vegetable oil. Saute for 4 minutes. Add the chicken broth, chicken, celery, carrots and sage to the pan. Stir until combined and bring the soup to a boil. Reduce the heat to medium low. Place a lid on the pan and simmer for 15 minutes or until the vegetables are tender.

In a mixing bowl, add the Bisquick, mashed potatoes, milk, green onion and black pepper. Stir until well combined and a soft dough forms. Drop the dough, by tablespoonfuls, onto the hot soup. Place a lid on the pan. Do not lift the lid and simmer for 20 minutes. A toothpick inserted in the center of the dumplings will come out clean when they are ready. Remove the pan from the heat and serve.

Buffalo Chicken Soup

This soup is so easy but so good! Goes great with chicken or turkey sandwiches. This is a perfect soup for a game watching party. No fuss and easy cleanup! Set the slow cooker to warm and guest can serve themselves when ready.

Makes 2 quarts

6 cups whole milk
3 cans cream of chicken soup, 10.75 oz. size
3 cups shredded cooked chicken
1 cup sour cream
1/2 cup Tabasco sauce

Add all the ingredients to a 4 quart slow cooker. Stir until combined. Set the temperature to low. Cook for 4 hours or until the soup is hot.

White Bean Chicken Chili

Makes 6 servings

12 oz. boneless skinless chicken breast, cubed
1/2 tsp. salt
1/4 tsp. black pepper
2 tbs. olive oil
1 cup chopped onion
4 garlic cloves, minced
1 jalapeno pepper, seeded & chopped
2 tsp. dried oregano
1 tsp. ground cumin
2 cans rinsed & drained cannellini beans, 15 oz. size
3 cups chicken broth
1 1/2 cups shredded cheddar cheese
1 cup sour cream

Sprinkle the chicken with salt and black pepper. In a large skillet over medium heat, add the olive oil. When the oil is hot, add the chicken. Saute for 2 minutes. Add the onion, garlic and jalapeno pepper to the skillet. Saute for 5 minutes. Sprinkle the oregano and cumin over the chicken and vegetables. Stir until combined. Remove the skillet from the heat.

Add the chicken and vegetables to a 4 quart slow cooker. In a small bowl, add 1 cup cannellini beans. Mash the beans with a fork. Add 1/2 cup chicken broth to the beans. Stir until combined and add to the slow cooker. Add the remaining beans and chicken broth to the slow cooker. Stir until combined.

Set the temperature to low. Cook for 3 hours or until the chicken is no longer pink and the chicken and vegetables are tender. Spoon the chili into bowls and sprinkle the cheddar cheese over the top. Spoon a dollop of sour cream over each serving.

Turkey Tortilla Soup

Makes 8 cups

10 corn tortillas, 6" size
1 cup chopped onion
2 garlic cloves, chopped
1 jalapeno pepper, seeded & minced
1 tbs. olive oil
4 cups chicken broth
10 oz. can enchilada sauce
2 cups chopped cooked turkey
1 tsp. ground cumin
1 avocado, peeled, pitted & cubed

Preheat the oven to 450°. Cut 5 corn tortillas into 1/2" strips. Spray the strips with non stick cooking spray. Place the strips, in a single layer, on a large baking sheet. Bake for 10 minutes or until browned. Stir every few minutes for even browning and to prevent burning. Remove from the oven and set aside.

In a dutch oven over medium heat, add the onion, garlic, jalapeno pepper and olive oil. Saute for 7 minutes or until tender. Cut 5 corn tortillas into 1/2" strips. Add the chicken broth and unbaked tortillas to the pan. Stir until combined and bring to a boil.

Add the enchilada sauce, turkey and cumin to the pan. Stir until combined and bring to a boil. Cook for 4 minutes. Remove the pan from the heat. Spoon the soup into bowls and sprinkle the avocado and baked tortillas over the top.

Turkey Meatball Soup

Makes 6 servings

3 cups cut fresh green beans
2 cups fresh baby carrots
2 cups chicken broth
1 tsp. dried oregano
1 tsp. dried basil
1 tsp. minced garlic
2 cans Italian stewed tomatoes, 15 oz. size
12 oz. pkg. refrigerated turkey meatballs
2 cups frozen whole kernel corn

In a dutch oven over medium heat, add the green beans, carrots, chicken broth, oregano, basil and garlic. Bring to a boil and reduce the heat to medium low. Place a lid on the pan. Simmer for 15 minutes or until the vegetables are tender.

Add the tomatoes with juice, meatballs and corn to the pan. Stir until combined. Place a lid on the pan. Simmer for 10 minutes or until the corn is tender and the meatballs hot. Remove from the heat and serve.

You can use fully cooked thawed frozen meatballs or leftover meatballs if desired.

Chicken Ratatouille Stew

Makes 8 servings

1 lb. boneless skinless chicken breast, cut into 1" pieces
26 oz. jar spaghetti sauce
1 eggplant, peeled & chopped
2 tomatoes, chopped
2 cups sliced zucchini
1 green bell pepper, cut into 1" pieces
3 garlic cloves, minced
1 tsp. dried basil
1 tsp. dried oregano
1/2 tsp. salt

Add all the ingredients to a 4 quart slow cooker. Stir until combined. Set the temperature to low. Cook for 6 hours or until the chicken and vegetables are tender.

3 HAM, BACON & PORK SOUPS & SANDWICHES

BLT's and barbecue sandwiches are the most popular pork sandwiches. Ham is a popular sandwich filling. I hope these recipes will inspire you to think outside the box for your next sandwich.

Savory Ham Wraps

Makes 4 servings

1/2 cup mayonnaise
2 tbs. whole milk
1/2 tsp. yellow prepared mustard
1/4 tsp. celery seed
1/8 tsp. salt
4 warm flour tortillas, 10" size
1/2 lb. cooked ham, thinly sliced
2/3 cup shredded Swiss cheese
1 1/3 cups shredded lettuce
2 tomatoes, seeded & chopped
2 green onions, chopped

In a small bowl, add the mayonnaise, milk, mustard, celery seed and salt. Stir until well combined. Spread the dressing over one side of each tortilla.

Place the ham over the dressing. Sprinkle the Swiss cheese, lettuce, tomato and green onions over the top. Tightly roll up and serve.

Deli Cristos

You can get most everything you need from the deli to make these delicious sandwiches.

Makes 2 servings

4 rye bread slices
4 oz. deli ham slices
4 oz. deli turkey slices
2 tbs. prepared coleslaw
2 tbs. Thousand Island dressing
2 Swiss cheese slices, 1 oz. size
2 eggs

Place 2 bread slices on your work surface. Place the ham and turkey over the bread slices. Spread the coleslaw and thousand island dressing over the meats. Place a Swiss cheese slice on top. Place the remaining bread slices over the sandwiches.

In a mixing bowl, add the eggs. Whisk until beaten. Spray a skillet with non stick cooking spray and place the skillet over medium heat. Dip each sandwich in the eggs allowing the excess liquid to drip off back in the bowl. Place the sandwiches in the skillet. Cook for 2-3 minutes on each side or until golden brown and the cheese melted. Remove the skillet from the heat and serve.

Grilled Ham & Chicken Salad Sandwiches

Makes 8 servings

1 1/3 cups finely chopped cooked ham
1 1/3 cups finely chopped cooked chicken
1/2 cup diced celery
8 oz. can crushed pineapple, drained
1/3 cup mayonnaise
3 tbs. chopped pecans
4 tsp. chopped green bell pepper
1 tsp. sliced green onion
1/4 tsp. salt
1/8 tsp. black pepper
16 slices Italian bread
8 slices mozzarella cheese, 1 oz. each
6 tbs. softened unsalted butter

In a mixing bowl, add the ham, chicken, celery, pineapple, mayonnaise, pecans, green bell pepper, green onion, salt and black pepper. Stir until well combined. Spread the chicken salad on one side of 8 bread slices. Place a mozzarella cheese slice over the filling on each sandwich. Place the remaining bread slices over the sandwiches.

Spread the butter on the outside slices of the bread on the sandwiches. In a large skillet over medium heat, add the sandwiches. Cook for 4 minutes on each side or until the bread is golden brown and the cheese melted. Remove the skillet from the heat and serve.

Cheddar Ham Breakfast Sandwiches

Makes 4 servings

4 slices frozen Texas Toast garlic bread, thawed
1 1/2 tsp. dried basil
1/2 tsp. dried rosemary
1 1/2 cups finely diced ham
1 1/2 cups shredded cheddar cheese

Preheat the oven to 400°. Place the garlic bread on a baking sheet. Sprinkle the basil and rosemary over the garlic bread. Sprinkle the ham and cheddar cheese over the bread. Bake for 10 minutes or until the garlic bread is golden brown and the cheese melted. Remove the pan from the oven and serve.

Fried Ham and Egg Salad Sandwiches

Makes 6 sandwiches

6 hard boiled eggs, peeled and chopped
1 cup diced cooked ham
1/2 cup diced celery
1 tbs. diced onion
1/2 cup mayonnaise
2 tsp. yellow prepared mustard
1 1/2 tsp. salt
1/4 tsp. black pepper
12 slices sandwich bread
1/2 cup plain yellow cornmeal
1/2 cup all purpose flour
1 tsp. baking powder
2 cups whole milk
2 eggs
Vegetable oil for frying

In a mixing bowl, add the hard boiled eggs, ham, celery, onion, mayonnaise, mustard, 1/2 teaspoon salt and black pepper. Stir until well combined. Spread the egg salad on 6 of the bread slices. Place the remaining bread slices over the top to form a sandwich.

In a mixing bowl, add the cornmeal, all purpose flour, 1 teaspoon salt, baking powder, milk and 2 eggs. Whisk until the batter is smooth and combined. Dip each sandwich in the batter allowing the excess liquid to drip off back into the bowl.

You will need to fry the sandwiches in batches. In a deep skillet over medium heat, add vegetable oil to a depth of 1/2" in the skillet. When the oil is hot, add the sandwiches. Cook for 3 minutes on each side or until the sandwiches are golden brown. Remove the sandwiches from the oil and drain on paper towels.

Bacon Bean Sandwiches

Makes 5 servings

5 Italian bread slices, toasted
15 oz. can pork and beans, drained
10 bacon strips, cooked and crumbled
5 thin onion slices
5 slices American cheese, 1 oz. each

Preheat the oven to 350°. Place the bread on a baking sheet. Spoon the pork and beans over the bread slices. Sprinkle the bacon over the beans. Place an onion slice over each sandwich. Place the American cheese over the top. Bake for 15 minutes or until the beans are bubbly and the cheese melted. Remove the sandwiches from the oven and serve.

Make Your Own Panini Bar

Breads

Raisin Nut Bread
French Bread
Slider Rolls or dinner rolls
Challah or brioche bread
Pumpernickel bread
Rye bread
Any hearty white or multigrain bread

Cheeses

Brie
Sharp white cheddar
Blue cheese
Gruyere
Swiss
Creamy goat cheese
Cream cheese

Spreads

Apple Butter
Coarse grained mustards
Herb butters for spreading on the outside of sandwiches
Fruit Preserves
Pepper Jelly
Flavored Aiolis or mayonnaise

Toppings

Caramelized Onions
Sauteed apples or pears
Sliced fresh fruit or vegetables
Dried fruits
Fresh herbs
Thinly sliced cooked or deli meats
Bacon
Smoked salmon
Chopped Nuts

Place the sandwiches on a panini grill and cook for 2-3 minutes or until the sandwiches are golden brown and hot.

Make Your Own Panini Bar cont'd

Example sandwiches

Brie cheese with apple butter and bacon on raisin walnut bread. Spread cinnamon butter on the outside of the bread. To make cinnamon butter, add 1 tsp. ground cinnamon to 1/3 cup softened unsalted butter. Stir until combined.

Creamy goat cheese with smoked salmon on white or Italian bread. Spread dill butter on the outside of the bread. To make dill butter, add 1 tablespoon fresh minced dill to 1/3 cup softened unsalted butter.

Blue cheese with caramelized onions and sauteed pears on brioche bread. Spread unsalted butter on the outside of the bread.

Gruyere cheese with stone ground mustard, ham, dried apricots and chopped pistachios on French bread. Spread unsalted butter on the outside of the bread.

Sharp white cheddar with honey mustard, apple slices and toasted pecans on dinner rolls. Spread unsalted butter on the outside of the bread.

Use your imagination to form your perfect sandwiches. These sandwiches go well with just about any vegetable soup.

Country Ham & Peach Panini

Makes 4 servings

8 ciabatta bread slices
4 tsp. Dijon mustard
Black pepper to taste
4 slices fontina cheese, 1 oz. size
4 oz. thinly sliced cooked country ham
2 peaches, pitted and sliced
4 tsp. honey, optional
1 tbs. olive oil

Spread one side of 4 bread slices with the Dijon mustard. Season with black pepper to taste. Place the fontina cheese and ham slices over the mustard. Place the peach slices over the top. Drizzle with honey if desired. Place the remaining bread slices over the sandwiches.

Brush the outside slices of the sandwiches with olive oil. Preheat your panini press or use a non stick grill pan. Cook on a panini press about 4 minutes. Place the grill pan over medium heat and add the sandwiches to the pan. Cook about 4 minutes on each side or until golden brown. Remove from the heat and serve.

Ham Salad Sandwiches

Makes 6 servings

1 1/2 cups finely chopped smoked cooked ham
1/2 cup finely chopped celery
1/3 cup mayonnaise
2 tbs. sweet pickle relish
1/4 tsp. salt
1/8 tsp. black pepper
12 slices buttered toast
6 lettuce leaves
2 tomatoes, thinly sliced

In a mixing bowl, add the ham, celery, mayonnaise, sweet pickle relish, salt and black pepper. Stir until combined and spread on one side of 6 toast slices. Place a lettuce leaf on each sandwich over the ham salad. Place the tomatoes over the lettuce on each sandwich. Place the remaining toast slices on the sandwiches and serve.

Ham Salad Croissants

Makes 8 servings

3 cups ground cooked ham
2 cups shredded cheddar cheese
2 celery ribs, diced
8 green onions, chopped
1/3 cup sunflower kernels
1/3 cup diced green bell pepper
1/3 cup chopped dill pickle
1/3 cup mayonnaise
1/3 cup sour cream
4 oz. jar diced red pimentos, drained
1 tsp. dry ranch salad dressing mix
1 tsp. black pepper
1 tsp. minced fresh parsley
8 lettuce leaves
8 croissants, split and toasted

In a mixing bowl, add the ham, cheddar cheese, celery, green onions, sunflower kernels, green bell pepper, dill pickle, mayonnaise, sour cream, red pimentos, ranch dressing mix, black pepper and parsley. Stir until combined.

Spread the salad over the bottom croissants. Place a lettuce leaf over the filling. Place the top on the croissants and serve.

Warm Ham Swiss Wraps

Makes 6 servings

6 flour tortillas, 10" size
1 lb. thinly sliced deli ham
2 cups shredded Swiss cheese
3 cups chopped lettuce
1 tomato, diced
1/2 cup diced cucumber
2 tbs. chopped green bell pepper
2 green onions, chopped
3/4 cup mayonnaise
3 tbs. whole milk
2 tsp. granulated sugar
1 tsp. yellow prepared mustard
1/2 tsp. celery seed

Preheat the oven to 350°. Place the ham slices over the tortillas. Sprinkle the Swiss cheese over the ham. Roll the tortillas up and place in a 11 x 7 casserole dish. Bake for 15 minutes or until the cheese melts. Remove the dish from the oven.

In a mixing bowl, add the lettuce, tomato, cucumber, green bell pepper and green onions. Stir until combined. In a small bowl, add the mayonnaise, milk, granulated sugar, mustard and celery seed. Stir until combined. Halfway unroll the wraps. Spoon the lettuce mixture over the unrolled part of the wrap. Spoon the mayonnaise spread over the vegetables. Roll the wraps back up and serve.

Ham Mango Wraps

Makes 6 servings

1/3 cup sour cream
1/3 cup mayonnaise
2 tbs. minced fresh basil
2 tbs. minced chives
1 tbs. lemon juice
1/8 tsp. salt
1/8 tsp. black pepper
3 cups cubed cooked ham
2 cups chopped mango
6 warm flour tortillas, 10" size

In a mixing bowl, add the sour cream, mayonnaise, basil, chives, lemon juice, salt and black pepper. Stir until combined. Add the ham and mango to the bowl. Stir until combined. Spoon the filling down the center of the tortillas. Roll up and serve.

Melted Avocado Club Sandwiches

Makes 4 servings

2 ripe avocados, mashed
1 tbs. fresh lime juice
1 tbs. mayonnaise
1 tbs. yellow prepared mustard
1/8 tsp. cayenne pepper
8 sandwich bread slices
8 oz. thinly sliced deli ham
8 oz. thinly sliced deli roast beef
4 tomato slices
8 bacon slices, cooked
4 provolone cheese slices, 1 oz. each
3 tbs. softened unsalted butter

In a small bowl, add the avocados, lime juice, mayonnaise, mustard and cayenne pepper. Stir until combined and spread on one side of 4 bread slices. Place the ham and roast beef over the spread. Place 1 tomato slice, 2 bacon slices and 1 provolone cheese slice over the meats on each sandwich.

Place the remaining bread slices over the sandwiches. Spread the butter on both sides of the outer bread slices. In a skillet over medium heat, add the sandwiches. Cook for 3 minutes on each side or until the sandwiches are toasted and the cheese melted. Remove the skillet from the heat and serve.

Grilled Sourdough Clubs

Makes 6 servings

12 slices sourdough bread
6 slices cheddar cheese, 1 oz. size
8 oz. cooked turkey breast, thinly sliced
1/4 tsp. garlic powder
1/4 tsp. black pepper
8 oz. cooked ham, thinly sliced
12 bacon slices, cooked and halved
2 tbs. unsalted butter, softened

Place 6 bread slices on your work surface. Place a slice of cheddar cheese over each bread slice. Place the turkey over the cheese. Sprinkle the garlic powder and black pepper over the turkey. Place the ham and bacon over the turkey. Place the remaining bread slices over the top.

Spread the butter on the outside bread slices. In a large skillet, add the sandwiches. Cook for 3 minutes on each side or until golden brown. Remove the skillet from the heat and serve.

Antipasto Po' Boys

Makes 4 servings

16 oz. loaf frozen garlic bread, thawed
1/4 cup creamy Parmesan salad dressing
2 tbs. grated Parmesan cheese
14 oz. can artichoke hearts, drained and chopped
1 cup diced tomatoes
5 oz. pkg. thinly sliced pepperoni
1/2 cup sliced black olives
1 cup shredded mozzarella cheese

Preheat the oven to 400°. Separate the garlic bread into halves. Place the garlic bread on a baking pan. Bake for 4 minutes. Remove the bread from the oven.

In a mixing bowl, add the Parmesan salad dressing, Parmesan cheese, artichokes and tomatoes. Stir until combined and spread over the garlic bread. Place the pepperoni over the garlic bread. Sprinkle the black olives and mozzarella cheese over the garlic bread.

Bake for 10 minutes or until the garlic bread is toasted. Remove the bread from the oven. Place one half of the garlic bread over the other half. Cut into slices and serve.

Prosciutto Tomato Sandwiches

Makes 4 sandwiches

8 slices frozen Texas Toast garlic bread
1/3 cup mayonnaise
1/4 cup crumbled blue cheese
2 cups arugula
4 oz. pkg. thinly sliced prosciutto
1 large tomato, cut into 4 slices
Black pepper to taste

Preheat the oven to 400°. Place the garlic bread slices on a baking sheet. Bake for 5 minutes or until the bread is toasted. Remove the pan from the oven. In a small bowl, stir together the mayonnaise and blue cheese. Spread the mixture on one side of each bread slice.

Place the arugula, prosciutto and tomato slices over the mayonnaise on 4 slices. Season to taste with black pepper. Place the remaining slices over the top and serve.

Prosciutto Fontina Bakes

Makes 4 servings

4 flatbread rounds, 6" size
6 oz. thinly sliced prosciutto
4 oz. thinly sliced fontina cheese
2 cups arugula
2 thin slices purple onion, separated into rings
2 tbs. balsamic vinegar
1/4 tsp. black pepper

Slice each flat bread round in half horizontally. Place the prosciutto on the bottom halves. Place the fontina cheese over the prosciutto. Place the arugula and onion over the top. Drizzle the balsamic vinegar over the lettuce. Sprinkle the black pepper over the top. Place the top halves on the sandwiches.

Preheat the oven to 300°. Wrap each sandwich in aluminum foil. Bake for 15 minutes or until the sandwiches are hot. Remove from the oven and serve. I have fixed these sandwiches on bread slices and spread butter on the outside slices like a grilled cheese. Place on a panini press or cook in a skillet until golden brown.

Apple Prosciutto Sandwiches

Makes 8 servings

1/4 cup olive oil
1/2 cup chopped walnuts
2 tbs. grated Parmesan cheese
2 tbs. minced fresh rosemary
12 oz. loaf focaccia bread
8 thin slices prosciutto
1 apple, sliced
6 oz. Brie cheese, rind removed and sliced

In a food processor, add the olive oil, walnuts, Parmesan cheese and rosemary. Process until the walnuts are finely chopped. Cut the focaccia bread in half lengthwise. Spread the rosemary dressing on the cut sides of the bread.

Layer the prosciutto, apple and Brie cheese over the bottom half of the bread. Place the top half on the sandwich. Cut into 4 quarters. In a large skillet over medium heat, add the sandwiches. Cook for 3 minutes on each side or until golden brown. Remove the skillet from the oven. Cut each sandwich in half and serve.

Cheesy Spinach Bacon Sandwiches

Makes 4 servings

16 oz. loaf frozen garlic bread, thawed
3 garlic cloves, minced
2 tbs. olive oil
16 oz. pkg. frozen chopped spinach, thawed
3/4 tsp. salt
1/4 tsp. black pepper
6 bacon slices, cooked and crumbled
1 1/2 cups shredded mozzarella cheese
1/4 cup shredded Parmesan cheese

Preheat the oven to 400°. Separate the garlic bread into halves. Place the garlic bread on a baking sheet. Bake for 4 minutes. Remove the bread from the oven.

In a skillet over medium heat, add the garlic and olive oil. Saute for 2 minutes. Add the spinach, salt and black pepper to the skillet. Saute for 4 minutes. Remove the skillet from the heat and stir in the bacon. Spoon the spinach over the garlic bread. Sprinkle the mozzarella and Parmesan cheese over the spinach. Bake for 5 minutes or until the garlic bread is toasted and the cheeses melted. Remove the bread from the oven. Cut into slices and serve.

Egg BLT With Avocado Tomato Relish

Makes 6 servings

1 cup grape tomatoes, halved
1 avocado, diced
1 tbs. chopped fresh basil
1 garlic clove, minced
2 tbs. olive oil
2 1/2 tsp. red wine vinegar
Salt and black pepper to taste
1/4 cup mayonnaise
6 Italian bread slices, toasted
3 cups arugula
12 thick bacon slices, cooked
6 fried eggs

In a small bowl, add the grape tomatoes, avocado, basil, garlic, olive oil and red wine vinegar. Whisk until combined and season to taste with salt and black pepper.

Spread the mayonnaise on one side of each bread slice and place on a serving platter. Place 1/2 cup arugula and 2 bacon slices over the mayonnaise on each sandwich. Place a fried egg over the top. Spoon the relish over the top and serve.

Breakfast Panini Sandwiches

These sandwiches were designed for a delicious breakfast but they are great any time of the day!

Makes 2 servings

6 bacon slices
2 tbs. plus 1 tsp. unsalted butter, softened
4 beaten eggs
4 sourdough bread slices, 3/4" thick
1/8 tsp. salt
1/8 tsp. black pepper
3 oz. Brie cheese, thinly sliced
8 thin apple slices
1/2 cup fresh baby spinach

In a skillet over medium heat, add the bacon. Cook for 7 minutes or until the bacon is crispy. Remove the bacon from the skillet and drain on paper towels. Drain all the grease from the skillet.

Add 1 teaspoon butter to the skillet. When the butter melts, add the eggs. Stir constantly and cook until the eggs are set and scrambled. Remove the skillet from the heat.

Place the eggs on 2 slices of sourdough bread. Sprinkle the salt and black pepper over the eggs. Place the bacon, Brie cheese, apple slices and spinach over the eggs. Place the remaining bread slices on top of the sandwiches.

Spread 2 tablespoons butter on the outside slices of the bread. You can place the sandwiches on a hot panini press and cook for 3 minutes or cook in a skillet. To cook in a skillet, place the skillet over medium heat. Add the sandwiches to the skillet. Press the sandwiches down with a spatula. Cook for 3 minutes on each side or until the sandwiches are golden brown. Remove the skillet from the heat and serve.

Egg Salad BLT's

Makes 6 servings

4 hard boiled eggs, chopped
1/2 cup finely chopped celery
1/3 cup mayonnaise
2 tbs. sweet pickle relish
1/4 tsp. salt
1/8 tsp. black pepper
12 slices buttered toast
6 lettuce leaves
2 tomatoes, thinly sliced
12 bacon slices, cooked

In a mixing bowl, add the eggs, celery, mayonnaise, sweet pickle relish, salt and black pepper. Stir until combined and spread on one side of 6 toast slices. Place a lettuce leaf on each sandwich over the egg salad. Place the tomatoes and 2 slices bacon over the lettuce on each sandwich. Place the remaining toast slices on the sandwiches and serve.

Guacamole BLT

Makes 4 sandwiches

1 cup prepared guacamole
8 bread slices, toasted
8 tomato slices, about 1/4" thick
Salt and black pepper to taste
1 cup arugula
16 thick cut bacon slices, cooked

Spread the guacamole on one side of each bread slice. Place 2 tomato slices over the guacamole on 4 bread slices. Season the tomatoes with salt and black pepper to taste. Spread the arugula over the tomatoes. Place 4 bacon slices on each sandwich. Place the remaining bread on the sandwiches with the guacamole side down and serve.

Delicious with Cheddar Cheese Soup.

Texas Toast BLT

Makes 4 sandwiches

4 slices Texas toast cheese garlic bread
1 cup chopped lettuce
16 slices thick cut bacon, cooked
4 tomato slices, 1/2" thick
Salt and black pepper to taste
4 jarred hot banana pepper rings

Preheat the oven to 400°. Place the garlic bread slices on a baking sheet. Bake for 5 minutes or until toasted. Remove from the oven. Sprinkle the lettuce over the bread. Place 4 bacon slices over each bread slice. Place a tomato slice over the bacon. Season to taste with salt and black pepper. Place the banana peppers over the top and serve.

Fresh Spinach & Bacon Sandwiches

Makes 6 servings

1 1/2 lbs. fresh spinach
3/4 cup mayonnaise
3/4 tsp. black pepper
1/2 tsp. garlic salt
12 slices sandwich bread
8 oz. bacon, cooked and crumbled

Remove the stems from the spinach and finely chop the spinach. In a small bowl, add the mayonnaise, black pepper and garlic salt. Stir until combined and spread on one side of each bread slice.

Place the spinach and bacon over 6 bread slices. Place the remaining slices over the top of the sandwiches and serve.

Bacon Caesar Mozzarella Panini

Makes 4 sandwiches

13 oz. can refrigerated pizza crust dough
4 tsp. basil pesto
1/4 cup bottled Caesar dressing
8 oz. fresh mozzarella cheese, sliced
1/4 tsp. black pepper
12 slices cooked bacon
2 tomatoes, cut into 4 slices each
8 large fresh basil leaves
1/4 cup unsalted butter, softened

Preheat the oven to 375°. Spray a 15 x 10 x 1 baking sheet with non stick cooking spray. Remove the pizza crust dough from the can. Press the dough evenly in the bottom of the pan. Bake for 12 minutes or until the pizza crust is lightly browned. Remove the pizza crust from the oven and cool for 15 minutes.

Cut the pizza crust in half lengthwise. Cut each half, crosswise, to cut 4 rectangles from each half. You will have 8 squares when finished. Spread the basil pesto on one side of 4 slices. Spread the Caesar dressing on one side of the remaining 4 slices.

Place the mozzarella slices over the Caesar dressing. Sprinkle the black pepper over the mozzarella slices. Place 3 bacon slices, 2 tomato slices and 2 basil leaves over the mozzarella cheese. Place the remaining slices, pesto side down, over the sandwiches.

Spread the butter over the outside crust of the sandwiches. Preheat your panini grill. Place the sandwiches on the grill and close the lid. Cook for 2 minutes or until the pizza crust is golden brown and crispy. Remove the sandwiches from the grill and serve.

You can melt the butter in a large skillet if desired. Add the sandwiches and press the sandwiches down with a large spatula. Cook for 2 minutes on each side or until the pizza crust is golden brown and crispy. Remove the sandwiches from the skillet and serve.

Open Face Pork Tenderloin Sandwiches

Makes 4 sandwiches

1/4 cup orange marmalade
2 tbs. Dijon mustard
1 tsp. olive oil
1 lb. pork tenderloin
4 French bread slices, 3/4" thick and toasted

In a small bowl, add the orange marmalade, Dijon mustard and olive oil. Stir until combined and brush over the pork tenderloin. Place the tenderloin on a baking sheet. Preheat the oven to 350°. Bake for 30 minutes or until the pork is tender and no longer pink. The internal temperature should reach at least 160° on a meat thermometer. Remove the tenderloin from the oven and cool for 5 minutes.

Place the French bread slices on a serving platter. Thinly slice the pork tenderloin. Place the slices over the French bread and serve.

Sweet & Spicy Pork, Onion & Apple Sandwiches

Makes 4 sandwiches

1 lb. pork tenderloin, thinly sliced
1 onion, thinly sliced
1 apple, thinly sliced
1 tbs. minced fresh ginger
1/2 tsp. dried crushed red pepper flakes
2 tbs. water
1/3 cup red currant jelly
1 tsp. soy sauce
4 large French rolls
4 lettuce leaves

Spray a large skillet with non stick cooking spray. Place the skillet over medium heat. When the skillet is hot, add the pork tenderloin slices. Cook for 4-5 minutes or until well browned. The pork will not be done at this point. Remove the pork from the skillet and drain on paper towels.

Add the onion, apple, ginger, red pepper flakes and water to the skillet. Saute for 7 minutes or until the apple and onion are golden brown. Add the pork back to the skillet. Add the red currant jelly and soy sauce to the skillet. Stir constantly and cook for 2-3 minutes or until the pork is no longer pink and the glaze thickens. Remove the skillet from the heat.

Cut a thin slice off the top of each French roll. Pull the bread from the bottom roll leaving about a 1/2" shell around the bread. Place a lettuce leaf in the bottom of each roll. Spoon the pork and sauce over the lettuce. Place the top on the sandwiches and serve.

Pork Tenderloin Sliders

Makes 20 sliders

2 pork tenderloins, about 1 1/4 lbs. each
1 tbs. olive oil
2 tsp. salt
1 tsp. black pepper
1/4 cup dark brown sugar
2 tbs. Dijon mustard
3 tbs. fresh thyme leaves
2 tbs. chopped fresh rosemary
20 slider buns

Preheat the oven to 400°. Rub the pork tenderloins with 1 tablespoon olive oil. Sprinkle the salt and black pepper over the tenderloins. In a small bowl, add the brown sugar, Dijon mustard, thyme and rosemary. Stir until combined and rub over the tenderloins.

Place the tenderloins on a wire rack in a baking pan. Bake for 30-35 minutes or until the temperature reaches 160° on a meat thermometer inserted in the thickest part of the tenderloins. Remove from the oven and let the tenderloins rest for 10 minutes before slicing. Cut into thin slices and place on the buns. Serve with your favorite condiments.

Italian Sausage Sandwiches

Makes 6 servings

1 1/2 lbs. Italian sausage links
1/2 cup onion, sliced & separated into rings
1 green bell pepper, cut into thin strips
1 red bell pepper, cut into thin strips
1 tsp. dried oregano
6 French rolls, 6" size
1 1/2 cups shredded provolone cheese

Cut the sausage links in half but do not cut all the way through the links. Spread the links apart. In a skillet over medium heat, add the links. Cook for 5 minutes on each side or until well browned and no longer pink. Remove the sausage links from the skillet and drain on paper towels. Drain off the excess grease in the skillet.

Add the onion, green bell pepper and red bell pepper to the skillet. Stir constantly and cook about 7 minutes or until the vegetables are tender. Add the oregano to the skillet. Saute for 2 minutes. Remove the skillet from the heat. Place the sausage links on the bottom of the French rolls. Spoon the onions and peppers over the top. Sprinkle the provolone cheese over the top. Place the top on the sandwiches and serve.

Kielbasa Supper Sandwiches

Makes 4 servings

1 lb. fully cooked kielbasa sausage link
1 red bell pepper, julienned
1 onion, halved and thinly sliced
3 tsp. unsalted butter
1 cup chopped tomato
4 tbs. spicy mustard
4 hoagie buns, split & toasted

Cut the sausage into 4 equal portions. Cut each portion in half lengthwise but do not cut all the way through. The sausage should lay flat but still be joined on each portion. In a skillet over medium heat, add the sausage. Add the red bell pepper, onion and butter to the skillet.

Saute for 8 minutes or until the vegetables are tender and the sausages are well browned. Remove the skillet from the heat. Sprinkle the tomato over the sausages. Spread the mustard on the cut side of the hoagie buns. Place a sausage over the bottom half of each sandwich. Spoon the vegetables over the sausages. Place the top on the sandwiches and serve.

Grilled Honey Mustard Brats

Makes 8 servings

1 cup honey mustard
1/4 cup mayonnaise
2 tsp. Worcestershire sauce
1/4 tsp. celery seed
8 uncooked bratwurst links
8 brat buns

In a small bowl, add the honey mustard, mayonnaise, Worcestershire sauce and celery seed. Stir until combined. Spoon 3/4 cup dressing into a Ziploc bag. Add the brats to the bag. Close the bag and shake until the brats are coated in the dressing. Refrigerate for 30 minutes. Refrigerate the remaining sauce for now.

Have your grill hot and ready. Spray the grill with non stick cooking spray. Remove the brats from the dressing. Discard the used dressing. Place the brats on the grill over medium coals or 350°. Close the lid on the grill and cook for 10 minutes. Turn the brats a few times while cooking.

Baste the brats with 2 tablespoons refrigerated dressing. Cook for 3 minutes or until the brats are done and browned. Brush the remaining dressing over the brat buns. Remove the brats from the grill and place in the buns.

Hearty Sausage Sandwich

Makes 6 servings

1 lb. ground Italian sausage
1 cup chopped onion
1/2 cup chopped green bell pepper
1 garlic clove, minced
8 oz. cream cheese, cubed
1/4 cup chopped fresh mushrooms
1/4 cup grated Parmesan cheese
1/4 cup water
1/4 tsp. dried oregano
1 lb. loaf unsliced Italian bread
1 1/2 cups shredded mozzarella cheese

In a large skillet over medium heat, add the Italian sausage, onion, green bell pepper and garlic. Stir frequently to break the sausage into crumbles as it cooks. Cook for 10 minutes or until the sausage is well browned and no longer pink. Drain off the excess grease.

Add the cream cheese, mushrooms, Parmesan cheese, water and oregano to the skillet. Stir constantly and cook about 5 minutes or until the cheeses melt and the filling thickens. Remove the skillet from the heat.

Cut the Italian bread in half horizontally. Remove the bread from both halves leaving about 3/4" shell on the loaves. Sprinkle 3/4 cup mozzarella cheese in the bottom loaf. Spoon the sausage filling in the bottom loaf over the cheese. Sprinkle the remaining mozzarella cheese over the top. Place the top on the sandwich and place the sandwich on a baking sheet.

Preheat the oven to 375°. Bake for 15 minutes or until the cheese melts and the sandwich is hot. Remove from the oven and cut into slices to serve.

Asparagus Prosciutto Sandwich

Makes 4 servings

1 lb. fresh asparagus, trimmed to 4" pieces
3/4 tsp. salt
16 oz. loaf French bread
2 tbs. unsalted butter, softened
4 plum tomatoes, sliced
1/8 tsp. black pepper
4 thin prosciutto slices
8 oz. fontina cheese, shredded

Place the asparagus in a sauce pan. Cover the asparagus with water and place the pan over medium heat. Cook about 5 minutes or until the asparagus is crisp tender. Remove the pan from the heat and drain all the water from the asparagus. Sprinkle 1/4 teaspoon salt over the asparagus and toss until combined.

Cut the French bread loaf in half horizontally. Brush the butter on the cut sides of the bread. Place the bread on a baking sheet. Preheat the oven to the broiler position. Broil for 2 minutes or until the bread is toasted. Remove the bread from the oven but leave the broiler on.

Place the tomato slices on each bread half. Sprinkle 1/2 teaspoon salt and black pepper over the tomatoes. Place the asparagus and prosciutto over the tomatoes. Sprinkle the fontina cheese over the top. Broil the sandwiches for 2 minutes or until the cheese is melted. Remove the sandwiches from the oven and serve.

French Club Sandwiches

Take these sandwiches to your next tailgating party.

Makes 6 servings

8 oz. container chive and onion cream cheese
2 tbs. mayonnaise
1 celery rib, chopped
1/2 cup shredded cheddar cheese
2 French baguettes, about 8 oz. each
1 lb. thinly sliced cooked ham
6 dill pickle stacker slices

In a mixing bowl, add the cream cheese, mayonnaise, celery and cheddar cheese. Stir until combined. Cut the baguettes in half lengthwise. Spread the cream cheese mixture on the cut sides of the bread. Place the ham on the bottom half of each baguette. Place the pickles over the ham. Place the top baguette half on the sandwiches. Cut each sandwich into slices before serving.

Bacon and Swiss Cheese Melts

Makes 5 sandwiches

1 cup shredded Swiss cheese
8 bacon slices, cooked and crumbled
1/4 cup mayonnaise
1 tbs. chopped fresh chives
1 tbs. grated onion
1/2 tsp. celery salt
1/8 tsp. cayenne pepper
10 slices bread
2 tbs. unsalted butter, softened

Preheat the oven to 325°. In a mixing bowl, add the Swiss cheese, bacon, mayonnaise, chives, onion, celery salt and cayenne pepper. Stir until well combined.

Spread the butter on one side of each bread slice. Place 5 bread slices, butter side down, on a baking sheet. Spread the cheese spread over the unbuttered side of the bread. Place the remaining bread slices, butter side up, over the spread.

Bake for 15 minutes or until the sandwiches are toasted and the cheese is melted. Remove the sandwiches from the oven and serve.

Italian Stuffed Sandwich

Makes 4 servings

16 oz. round loaf Italian bread
8 bacon slices, chopped
2/3 cup chopped onion
2 garlic cloves, minced
14 oz. jar artichoke hearts, drained and chopped
3/4 cup shredded Parmesan cheese
1/3 cup mayonnaise
1/4 cup minced fresh parsley
1/4 tsp. black pepper
16 oz. jar marinara sauce
1/3 cup dry white wine

Cut off the top third of the bread loaf and set aside. Remove the inside bread from the loaf leaving about 1/4" thick shell on the loaf. Tear the bread into small pieces and set aside.

In a skillet over medium heat, add the bacon. Cook about 8 minutes or until the bacon is crisp. Remove the bacon from the skillet and drain on paper towels. Crumble the bacon into pieces. Leave the bacon drippings in the skillet.

Add the onion and 1 garlic clove to the skillet. Saute the vegetables for 5 minutes or until they are tender. Drain off the excess grease. Add the torn bread pieces, bacon, artichokes, 1/2 cup Parmesan cheese, mayonnaise, 2 tablespoons parsley and black pepper to the skillet. Stir until combined and remove the skillet from the heat. Spoon the filling into the bottom bread loaf.

Place the removed top on the sandwich. Wrap the sandwich in aluminum foil. Preheat the oven to 375°. Bake the sandwich for 20 minutes. Unwrap the sandwich and remove the top slice. Sprinkle 1/4 cup Parmesan cheese over the sandwich. Place the top slice back on the sandwich and bake for 5 minutes. Remove the sandwich from the oven and cut into slices.

In a sauce pan over medium heat, add 1 garlic clove and the marinara sauce. Stir until combined and bring the sauce to a boil. Reduce the heat to low and simmer for 10 minutes. Stir occasionally while the sauce simmers. Stir in the white wine and simmer for 5 minutes. Remove the pan from the heat and stir in 2 tablespoons parsley. Serve the sandwich with the sauce.

Grilled Ham & Asparagus Sandwiches

Makes 4 servings

2 tbs. plus 4 tsp. unsalted butter, softened
2 tbs. all purpose flour
1 cup whole milk
1 cup shredded sharp cheddar cheese
8 slices sandwich bread
8 slices cooked deli ham
4 thin slices onion
4 thick slices tomato
16 cooked asparagus spears, ends trimmed
4 slices American cheese

In a sauce pan over medium heat, add 2 tablespoons butter. When the butter melts, stir in the all purpose flour. Stir constantly and cook for 1 minute. Keep stirring and add the milk. Stir constantly and cook until the sauce thickens and bubbles. Remove the pan from the heat and stir in the sharp cheddar cheese. Stir until the cheese melts. Keep the cheese sauce warm while you make the sandwiches.

Butter one side of each bread slice with 1/2 teaspoon butter. Place 4 slices bread, buttered side down, on a hot griddle. Add 2 slices ham to each bread slice. Place 1 slice onion, 1 slice tomato, 4 asparagus spears and 1 slice American cheese over the ham. Top the sandwich with the remaining bread slices. The top slices should be buttered side up.

Cook about 3 minutes on each side or until the sandwiches are golden brown and the ham hot. Remove the sandwiches from the griddle on place on a serving plate. Pour the cheese sauce over the sandwiches when ready to serve.

Ham & Cheese Loaf

Makes 8 servings

1 lb. loaf sourdough bread
1 cup sliced fresh mushrooms
1 green bell pepper, cut into thin strips
1 red bell pepper, cut into thin strips
1 celery rib, sliced
3 green onions, sliced
2 tbs. olive oil
1/2 cup mayonnaise
2 tsp. dried Italian seasoning
1/2 tsp. black pepper
1 lb. cooked ham, thinly sliced
1 cup shredded colby cheese
1/2 cup shredded mozzarella cheese

Cut the bread in half horizontally. Remove the bread from the top and bottom pieces leaving about 1/2" bread on the shells. Use the removed bread for another recipe or discard.

In a large skillet over medium heat, add the mushrooms, green bell pepper, red bell pepper, celery, green onions and olive oil. Saute for 5 minutes or until the vegetables are tender. Remove the skillet from the heat.

In a small bowl, add the mayonnaise, Italian seasoning and black pepper. Spread the mayonnaise on the cut side of the bread shells. Place half the ham in the bottom bread shell. Spoon half the vegetables over the ham. Sprinkle 1/2 cup colby cheese and 1/4 cup mozzarella cheese over the top. Repeat the layering process one more time.

Place the top bread shell on the sandwich. Wrap the sandwich in aluminum foil and place on a baking sheet. Preheat the oven to 400°. Bake for 30 minutes or until the sandwich is hot. Remove from the oven and cut into wedges to serve.

Tomato, Swiss and Bacon Sandwiches

Makes 4 sandwiches

1 tbs. unsalted butter
8 Canadian bacon slices
3 tbs. mayonnaise
1/2 tsp. fresh dill, minced
8 slices multigrain bread
1 large tomato, cut into 8 slices
1/4 tsp. salt
1/2 tsp. black pepper
4 slices Swiss cheese, about 1 oz. each
4 lettuce leaves

In a skillet over medium heat, add the butter. When the butter melts, add the Canadian bacon. Cook the bacon about 3 minutes on each side or until the bacon is browned. Remove the skillet from the heat. Drain the bacon on paper towels.

In a small bowl, add the mayonnaise and dill. Stir until well combined and spread the mayonnaise on one side of the bread slices. Place 2 bacon slices over the mayonnaise. Place 2 tomato slices over the bacon. Sprinkle the salt and black pepper over the tomatoes. Place the Swiss cheese and lettuce over the tomatoes. Top with the remaining bread slices and serve.

Grilled Pizza Pesto Sandwiches

Makes 4 servings

6 oz. pkg. sliced mozzarella cheese
8 slices Italian Bread, 1" thick
1/4 cup pizza sauce
1/4 cup pesto sauce
20 slices pepperoni
2 tbs. softened unsalted butter

Place one mozzarella cheese slice on the top of 4 Italian bread slices. Spread the pizza sauce over the cheese. Place another mozzarella cheese slice over the sauce. Spread the pesto sauce over the cheese. Place the pepperoni slices over the top. Place the remaining bread slices over top of the sandwiches.

Spread the butter on the outside slices of the sandwiches. In a large skillet over medium heat, add the sandwiches. Cook for 3-4 minutes on each side or until the cheese melts and the sandwiches are golden brown. Remove the skillet from the heat and serve.

Po Boy Loaf

Makes 8 servings

12 oz. loaf unsliced Italian bread
1/4 cup unsalted butter, softened
1 tbs. stone ground mustard
1 tbs. minced fresh parsley
1 garlic clove, minced
1/8 tsp. crushed red pepper flakes
2 tomatoes, thinly sliced
6 oz. mozzarella cheese, thinly sliced
6 oz. hard salami, thinly sliced
1/3 cup banana pepper rings

Cut the bread into 1/2" slices but do not cut all the way through to the bottom of the loaf. The loaf needs to stay intact. In a small bowl, add the butter, mustard, parsley, garlic and red pepper flakes. Stir until combined. Spread the butter on every other slice of the bread. Place the tomatoes, mozzarella cheese, salami and banana peppers in the unbuttered slices.

Preheat the oven to 350°. Wrap the loaf in aluminum foil. Bake for 15 minutes or until the cheese melts and the sandwich is warm. Remove from the oven and serve.

Italian Salami Loaf

Makes 4 sandwiches

4 French sandwich loaves
1/4 cup olive oil
1 tbs. red wine vinegar
2 tomatoes, thinly sliced
1 cup thinly sliced cucumber
8 oz. provolone cheese, sliced
2 cups thinly sliced salami
1 onion, thinly sliced & separated into rings
3 tbs. chopped fresh parsley
1/8 tsp. dried basil
1/4 tsp. black pepper
1 garlic clove, minced

Cut each French loaf in half horizontally. Brush 1 tablespoon olive oil on the cut sides of the bread. In a small bowl, add the remaining olive oil and red wine vinegar. Whisk until combined.

Place the tomatoes on the bottom half of the bread. Brush the tomatoes with the oil and vinegar dressing. Place the cucumbers over the tomatoes. Brush the cucumbers with the oil and vinegar dressing. Place the provolone cheese, salami and onion over the cucumbers. Brush the top with the oil and vinegar dressing.

In a small bowl, add the parsley, basil, black pepper and garlic. Stir until combined and sprinkle over the top of the sandwiches. Place the top on the sandwiches. Wrap each sandwich in plastic wrap. Let the sandwiches sit for 30 minutes at room temperature before serving.

Ham Black Bean Potato Soup

Makes 6 servings

15 oz. can black beans, rinsed and drained
2 cups diced peeled potatoes
8 oz. cooked ham, diced
6 cups beef broth
1/4 cup dried minced onion
4 oz. can diced jalapeno peppers, drained
1 garlic clove, minced
1 tsp. ground cumin
1 tsp. dried oregano
1 tsp. dried thyme
1/8 tsp. ground cloves

Add all the ingredients to a 4 quart slow cooker. Stir until combined. Set the temperature to low and cook for 8 hours.

Ham & Bean Soup

Makes 10 servings

1 lb. dried navy beans
2 cups chopped onion
2 tsp. vegetable oil
2 celery ribs, chopped
10 cups water
4 cups cubed cooked ham
1 cup mashed potatoes
1/2 cup shredded carrot
2 tbs. Worcestershire sauce
1 tsp. salt
1/2 tsp. dried thyme
1/2 tsp. black pepper
2 bay leaves
1 meaty ham bone
1/4 cup minced fresh parsley

In a dutch oven over medium heat, add the navy beans. Cover the beans with water to 2" above the beans. Bring the beans to a boil and boil for 2 minutes. Remove the pan from the heat and place a lid on the pan. Let the beans sit for 1 hour.

Drain the water from the beans. In a sauce pan over medium heat, add the onion and vegetable oil. Saute for 4 minutes. Add the celery to the pan. Saute for 3 minutes. Remove the pan from the heat and add to the beans. Add 10 cups water, ham, potatoes, carrot, Worcestershire sauce, salt, thyme, black pepper, bay leaves and ham bone to the beans. Stir until combined.

Place the pan on the stove over medium heat. Bring to a boil and reduce the heat to medium low. Place a lid on the pan. Stir occasionally and cook about 1 1/2 hours or until the beans are tender. Remove the pan from the heat. Remove the bay leaves and discard. Remove the ham bone from the soup. Remove the ham from the bone and add the meat back to the soup. Stir until combined. Spoon into bowls and sprinkle the parsley over the top.

Ham Bone Split Pea Soup

Makes 1 gallon

1 lb. pkg. dried green split peas
2 quarts water
1 cup chopped onion
1 potato, peeled & diced
1 cup chopped celery
1 meaty ham bone
1 garlic clove, minced
1 tsp. salt
1/4 tsp. black pepper
1 bay leaf
2 cups chopped carrots

Rinse the green peas and remove any bad peas. Add the peas to a dutch oven. Add cold water until the water is about 2" above the peas. Place a lid on the pan and soak the peas for 12 hours.

Drain the water from the peas. Add 2 quarts water, onion, potato, celery, ham bone, garlic, salt, black pepper, bay leaf and carrots to the peas. Place the pan over medium heat and bring to a boil. Place a lid on the pan. Stir frequently and simmer about 2 1/4 hours or until the peas are tender. Remove the pan from the heat.

Remove the bay leaf and discard. Remove the ham bone from the soup. Cut any remaining ham on the bone and add to the soup. Using a hand blender, puree the soup to your desired taste. Serve hot.

Cheddar Ham Soup

Makes 7 servings

2 cups diced peeled potatoes
2 cups water
1/2 cup sliced carrot
1/4 cup chopped onion
1/4 cup unsalted butter, cubed
1/4 cup all purpose flour
2 cups whole milk
1/2 tsp. salt
1/4 tsp. black pepper
2 cups shredded cheddar cheese
1 1/2 cups cubed cooked ham
1 cup frozen green peas, thawed

In a sauce pan over medium heat, add the potatoes, water, carrot and onion. Bring to a boil and reduce the heat to low. Simmer for 15 minutes or until the vegetables are tender.

While the vegetables are cooking, make the sauce. In a sauce pan over medium heat, add the butter. When the butter melts, add the all purpose flour. Stir constantly and cook for 2 minutes. Add the milk, salt and black pepper to the pan. Stir constantly and cook about 4 minutes or until the sauce thickens and bubbles. Remove the pan from the heat and add the cheddar cheese. Stir until the cheese melts and add to the vegetables.

Add the ham and green peas to the soup. Stir until combined and cook about 4 minutes or until the peas are tender. Remove the pan from the heat and serve.

Italian Wedding Soup

Makes 2 1/2 quarts

2 beaten eggs
1/2 cup seasoned breadcrumbs
1 lb. ground beef
1 lb. ground Italian sausage
3 carrots, sliced
3 celery ribs, diced
1 1/4 cups chopped onion
3 garlic cloves, minced
4 1/2 tsp. olive oil
10 oz. pkg. frozen chopped spinach, thawed
4 cans chicken broth, 14 oz. size
1/4 cup minced fresh basil
1 envelope dry onion soup mix
4 1/2 tsp. ketchup
1/2 tsp. dried thyme
3 bay leaves
1 1/2 cups penne pasta

In a mixing bowl, add the eggs, breadcrumbs, ground beef and Italian sausage. Using your hands, mix until well combined. Form the meat into meatballs about 3/4" in size.

Preheat the oven to 350°. Line a large baking sheet with aluminum foil. Place the meatballs on the baking sheets. Bake for 15-18 minutes or until the meatballs are no longer pink and browned. Remove from the oven.

While the meatballs are cooking, make the soup. In a dutch oven over medium heat, add the carrots, celery, onion, garlic and olive oil. Saute for 10 minutes. Pat the spinach dry with paper towels. Add the spinach, chicken broth, basil, onion soup mix, ketchup, thyme and bay leaves to the pan. Stir until combined and bring to a boil.

Add the meatballs to the soup. Reduce the heat to low and simmer for 30 minutes. Add the penne pasta to the soup. Cook for 12 minutes or until the pasta is tender. Remove the pan from the heat and serve.

Southwestern Green Chile Sausage Soup

Makes 6 servings

2 cans drained green chiles, 4 oz. size
1/4 cup fresh cilantro, chopped
2 garlic cloves, minced
1 tsp. ground cumin
1/8 tsp. salt
12 oz. cooked smoked sausage, finely chopped
2 tsp. olive oil
1/4 cup chopped green onions
2 cans chicken broth, 14 oz. size
2 cans drained white shoe peg corn, 11 oz. size
1 cup frozen green peas
3 cups shredded cabbage
3/4 cup shredded Monterey Jack cheese
1 lime, cut into 6 wedges

In a blender, add the green chiles, cilantro, garlic and cumin. Process until smooth and combined. Spoon the salsa into a bowl. Add the salt and stir until combined.

In a dutch oven over medium heat, add the sausage and olive oil. Saute for 6 minutes or until the sausage is well browned. Add the green onions, chicken broth, corn and green peas. Stir until combined and bring to a boil. Reduce the heat to low.

Reserve 1/4 cup salsa and set aside. Add the remaining salsa to the pan. Stir until combined and simmer for 5 minutes. Remove the pan from the heat.

Place the cabbage into bowls. Sprinkle the Monterey Jack cheese over the cabbage. Spoon the soup over the cabbage. Spoon the remaining 1/4 cup salsa over the top of each serving. Squeeze a lime wedge across the soup and serve.

Spicy Cajun Corn Soup

Makes 10 servings

1/2 cup vegetable oil
1/2 cup all purpose flour
1 cup finely chopped onion
1 cup finely chopped green bell pepper
6 green onions, chopped
2 cups chopped fresh tomatoes
15 oz. can diced tomatoes
6 oz. can tomato paste
3 cups water
1 1/2 lbs. cooked smoked sausage, cut into 1/2" slices
3 cups diced cooked ham
2 pkgs. frozen whole kernel corn, 1 lb. size
1 tsp. salt
1/2 tsp. crushed red pepper flakes
1/2 tsp. cayenne pepper
1/2 tsp. Tabasco sauce

In a heavy dutch oven over medium heat, add the vegetable oil. When the oil is hot, add the all purpose flour. Whisk constantly and cook for 5 minutes or until the flour is golden brown. Add the onion, green bell pepper and green onions to the pan. Stir constantly and cook for 6 minutes.

Add the tomatoes, canned tomatoes with juice, tomato paste, water, smoked sausage, ham, corn, salt, red pepper flakes, cayenne pepper and Tabasco sauce. Stir until combined and bring to a boil. Reduce the heat to low. Partially cover the pan with a lid. Stir occasionally and simmer for 1 hour. Remove the pan from the heat and serve.

Sausage Bean Soup

Makes 10 servings

4 cups water
1 potato, peeled & chopped
6 brown & serve sausage links
2 cans rinsed & drained red kidney beans, 15 oz. size
28 oz. can diced tomatoes
1 cup chopped onion
1 green bell pepper, chopped
1 bay leaf
1/2 tsp. garlic salt
1/2 tsp. season salt
1/2 tsp. black pepper
1/2 tsp. dried thyme

In a large sauce pan over medium heat, add the water and potato. Bring to a boil and reduce the heat to medium low. Simmer for 10 minutes or until the potato is tender.

While the potato is cooking, brown the sausage. Crumble the links into the skillet over medium heat. Stir frequently and cook for 5 minutes or until the sausage is well browned. Remove the skillet from the heat and add to the potatoes.

Add the kidney beans, tomatoes with juice, onion, green bell pepper, bay leaf, garlic salt, season salt, black pepper and thyme to the pan. Stir until combined. Simmer for 10 minutes or until the soup is thoroughly heated. Remove the pan from the heat and serve.

Italian Root Vegetable Soup

Makes about 1 gallon

1/4 lb. ground Italian sausage
3 lb. butternut squash, peeled & cubed
4 large peeled potatoes, diced
3 large sweet potatoes, peeled & cubed
1 large rutabaga, peeled & cubed
1 lb. pkg. fresh baby carrots
1 turnip, peeled & diced
10 cups water
2 cans vegetable broth, 14 oz. size
2 tbs. granulated sugar
1 1/2 tsp. salt
1 tsp. ground ginger
1/8 tsp. black pepper
1/4 heavy whipping cream

In a soup pot over medium heat, add the Italian sausage. Stir frequently to break the sausage into crumbles as it cooks. Cook for 7 minutes or until the sausage is well browned and no longer pink. Drain off the excess grease.

Add the butternut squash, potatoes, sweet potatoes, rutabaga, carrots, turnip, water, vegetable broth, granulated sugar, salt, ginger and black pepper to the pan. Stir until combined and bring to a boil. Reduce the heat to medium low and place a lid on the pan. Simmer for 40-45 minutes or until the vegetables are tender.

Using a hand blender, puree the soup. Add the whipping cream to the pan. Stir until combined and cook for 2 minutes. Remove the soup from the heat and serve.

Creamy Bacon Mushroom Soup

Makes 2 quarts

10 bacon strips, diced
1 lb. sliced fresh mushrooms
1 cup chopped onion
3 garlic cloves, minced
1 quart heavy whipping cream
14 oz. can chicken broth
5 oz. shredded Swiss cheese
3 tbs. cornstarch
1/2 tsp. salt
1/2 tsp. black pepper
3 tbs. water

In a dutch oven over medium heat, add the bacon. Cook about 8 minutes or until the bacon is crisp. Remove the bacon from the pan using a slotted spoon and drain on paper towels.

Drain all but 2 tablespoons bacon drippings from the pan. Add the mushrooms, onion and garlic to the pan. Saute for 10 minutes or until the vegetables are tender. Add the heavy whipping cream, chicken broth and Swiss cheese to the pan. Stir until the cheese melts.

In a small bowl, add the cornstarch, salt, black pepper and water. Whisk until combined and add to the soup. Stir constantly and bring the soup to a boil. Cook for 2 minutes or until the soup thickens. Remove the pan from the heat and stir in the bacon.

Cheesy Bacon Corn Chowder

Makes 3 1/2 quarts

6 bacon slices, chopped
3/4 cup chopped onion
2 1/2 cups water
2 1/2 cups potatoes, peeled & diced
2 cups sliced fresh carrots
2 tsp. instant chicken bouillon granules
3 cans drained gold & white corn, 11 oz. size
1/2 tsp. black pepper
7 tbs. all purpose flour
5 cups whole milk
3 cups shredded cheddar cheese
1 cup cubed Velveeta cheese

In a large dutch oven over medium heat, add the bacon and onion. Saute for 6 minutes or until the bacon is crispy. Add the water, potatoes, carrots and chicken bouillon to the pan. Stir until combined and bring to a boil. Reduce the heat to medium low. Place a lid on the pan and simmer for 15 minutes or until the potatoes are tender.

Add the corn and black pepper to the pan. Stir until combined. In a mixing bowl, add the all purpose flour and milk. Whisk until combined and add to the pan. Stir constantly and cook for 2 minutes or until the chowder thickens. Add the cheddar cheese and Velveeta cheese to the pan. Stir until the cheese melts. Remove the pan from the heat and serve.

Pancetta Cheese Tortellini Soup

Makes 8 servings

2 tbs. olive oil
4 oz. pancetta, finely chopped
1 cup finely chopped onion
3 garlic cloves, minced
6 1/4 cups chicken broth
2 tsp. dried Italian seasoning
9 oz. pkg. refrigerated cheese tortellini
28 oz. can crushed tomatoes
8 oz. fresh baby spinach, chopped
Salt and black pepper to taste
1 cup freshly shredded Parmesan cheese

In a dutch oven over medium heat, add the olive oil. When the oil is hot, add the pancetta. Saute for 5 minutes or until the pancetta is crisp. Add the onion to the pan. Saute for 4 minutes. Add the garlic to the pan. Saute for 2 minutes.

Add the chicken broth and Italian seasoning to the pan. Stir until combined and bring to a boil. Simmer for 3 minutes. Add the cheese tortellini and crushed tomatoes to the soup. Stir until combined and cook for 4 minutes or until the tortellini is done. Add the spinach to the soup. Cook for 1 minute or until the spinach wilts. Remove the pan from the heat. Season to taste with salt and black pepper. Spoon into bowls and sprinkle the Parmesan cheese over the top.

Stir Fried Pork Soup

Makes 6 servings

12 oz. boneless pork loin, cut into thin strips
1 cup sliced fresh mushrooms
1 cup chopped celery
1/2 cup diced carrots
2 tbs. vegetable oil
6 cups chicken broth
1/2 cup chopped fresh spinach
2 tbs. cornstarch
3 tbs. cold water
1 beaten egg
Black pepper to taste

In a dutch oven over medium heat, add the pork loin, mushrooms, celery, carrots and vegetable oil. Saute for 8 minutes or until the pork is no longer pink and the vegetables tender.

Add the chicken broth and spinach to the pan. In a small bowl, add the cornstarch and water. Whisk until combined and add to the soup. Stir constantly and bring to the soup to a boil. Boil for 1 minute. Whisk the beaten egg into the soup. Remove the pan from the heat and season to taste with black pepper.

Spicy Pork Chili

Makes 2 1/2 quarts

1 lb. ground pork
3 cups chopped onion
4 garlic cloves, minced
1 red bell pepper, chopped
1 green bell pepper, chopped
1 cup chopped celery
2 cans diced tomatoes, 14 oz. size
15 oz. can red kidney beans, rinsed & drained
6 oz. can tomato paste
3/4 cup water
2 tsp. light brown sugar
1 tsp. dried oregano
1 tsp. chili powder
1/4 tsp. dried red pepper flakes
1/4 tsp. cayenne pepper
1/8 tsp. Tabasco sauce

In a dutch oven over medium heat, add the pork and onions. Stir frequently to break the pork into crumbles as it cooks. Cook for 8 minutes or until the pork is no longer pink and tender. Drain off the excess grease.

Add the garlic, red bell pepper, green bell pepper and celery to the pan. Saute for 5 minutes. Add the tomatoes with juice, red kidney beans, tomato paste, water, brown sugar, oregano, chili powder, red pepper flakes, cayenne pepper and Tabasco sauce to the pan. Stir until combined and place a lid on the pan.

Reduce the heat to low. Stir occasionally and simmer for 45 minutes. Remove the pan from the heat and serve.

4 EGG & CHEESE SOUPS & SANDWICHES

Everyone loves grilled cheese sandwiches and I have included all our favorite versions. Cheese soup is a must on a cold winters day.

Herb Cheese Sandwiches with Artichoke Salsa

Makes 8 sandwiches

2 tomatoes, chopped
14 oz. jar artichoke hearts, drained and chopped
2 tsp. olive oil
2 garlic cloves, minced
3 tbs. chopped fresh basil
15 oz. carton ricotta cheese
7 oz. pkg. crumbled feta cheese
1/2 cup chopped fresh parsley
1 tsp. chopped fresh dill
16 rye bread slices

In a serving bowl, add the tomatoes, artichokes, olive oil, garlic and basil. Stir until combined. Cover the bowl and refrigerate until the salsa is chilled.

In a mixing bowl, add the ricotta cheese, feta cheese, parsley and dill. Stir until well combined and spread on one side of each bread slice. When the salsa is chilled, drain all the liquid from the salsa. Spoon the salsa on eight bread slices over the ricotta cheese. Place the remaining bread slices, ricotta cheese side down, over the top of the sandwiches and serve.

Deviled Egg Sandwiches

Makes 4 sandwiches

4 hard boiled eggs, chopped
2 oz. can deviled ham
3 tbs. mayonnaise
1 tsp. lemon juice
1/2 tsp. yellow prepared mustard
1/4 tsp. onion powder
8 slices pumpernickel bread
1 green bell pepper, thinly sliced

In a mixing bowl, add the hard boiled eggs, deviled ham, mayonnaise, lemon juice, mustard and onion powder. Stir until combined and spread on one side of 4 bread slices. Place the green bell pepper slices over the top. Place the remaining bread on the sandwiches and serve.

Fried Egg BBQ Bacon Sandwich

Makes 4 servings

5 tbs. light brown sugar
1 tbs. chili powder
1 tsp. ground cumin
1/4 tsp. cayenne pepper
12 slices thick cut bacon
3 1/2 tbs. melted unsalted butter
4 eggs
8 Texas toast bread slices
4 American cheese slices, 1 oz. each
1/4 cup mayonnaise
2 cups chopped lettuce

Preheat the oven to 350°. In a shallow bowl, add the brown sugar, chili powder, cumin and cayenne pepper. Stir until combined. Spray a large baking sheet with non stick cooking spray. Dredge the bacon slices in the brown sugar coating. Place the bacon slices on a baking sheet. Bake for 40 minutes or until the bacon is crispy. Remove the bacon from the oven and drain the bacon on paper towels.

In a skillet over medium heat, add 1 tablespoon butter. When the butter is hot, break 4 eggs into the skillet. Cook for 2 minutes on each side or until the fried eggs are done to your taste. Some people like the yolk cooked and some do not. Cook the eggs to your taste.

Brush both sides of the bread with 2 1/2 tablespoons butter. Preheat the oven to the broiler position. Place the bread slices on a baking pan. Broil for 2 minutes on each side or until the bread is toasted. Remove the bread from the oven and immediately place 1 American cheese slice on 4 slices of the bread.

Place 3 bacon strips over the cheese on each bread slice. Spread one side of the remaining bread slices with mayonnaise. Place a fried egg over the bacon on each sandwich. Sprinkle 1/2 cup lettuce over the egg on each sandwich. Place the remaining bread slices, mayonnaise side down. over the sandwiches and serve.

Garlic Bread Grilled Cheese

Makes 4 sandwiches

8 slices frozen Texas Toast garlic bread
8 oz. American cheese, sliced

Preheat the oven to 400°. Place the garlic bread slices on a baking sheet. Bake for 5 minutes. Remove the garlic bread from the oven. Place the American cheese slices over 4 garlic bread slices. Place the remaining bread slices over the cheese.

Bake for 5 minutes or until the cheese melts. Remove the sandwiches from the oven and serve.

Note: You can use your favorite cheese instead of the American cheese. We like to use Brie cheese and serve with Leek Soup.

Grilled Ham & Jack Cheese

Makes 4 servings

4 tbs. unsalted butter, softened
8 slices Texas toast
4 sharp cheddar cheese slices, 1 oz. size
12 oz. cooked ham, thinly sliced
4 thin purple onion slices
4 tbs. prepared ranch salad dressing
4 slices Pepper Jack cheese, 1 oz. size

Spread the butter on one side of each Texas toast slice. On the unbuttered side of 4 bread slices, place a slice of cheddar cheese. Place the ham over the cheese. Place the purple onion over the ham. Spread the ranch dressing on the unbuttered side of the remaining bread slices. Place a Pepper Jack cheese slice over the dressing. Place the bread slices, buttered side up, over the sandwiches.

In a large skillet over medium heat, add the sandwiches. Cook for 3 minutes on each side or until golden brown and the cheeses melt. Remove the skillet from the heat and serve.

Grilled Cheese Hoagies

Makes 6 servings

3/4 cup unsalted butter, softened
1 envelope dry Italian salad dressing mix
6 hoagie buns, split
1 lb. your favorite sandwich meat (ham, turkey, salami, etc)
12 Swiss cheese slices, 1 oz. size
6 hoagie buns, split

In a small bowl, add the butter and Italian salad dressing mix. Stir until combined and spread half the butter on the cut sides of the buns. Place the sandwich meat over the bottom buns. Place 2 Swiss cheese slices on each sandwich over the meat. Place the tops on the sandwiches.

Spread the remaining butter on the outside slices of the buns. In a large skillet over medium heat, add the sandwiches. Cook for 3 minutes on each side or until the cheese melts and the buns are golden brown. Remove from the heat and serve.

Grilled Parmesan, Tomato & Cheese Sandwiches

Makes 4 sandwiches

1/3 cup mayonnaise
1/3 cup grated Parmesan cheese
Black pepper to taste
8 Italian bread slices
8 provolone cheese slices, 1 oz. size
8 fresh tomato slices, 1/4" thick

In a small bowl, add the mayonnaise and Parmesan cheese. Stir until combined. Season to taste with black pepper. Place 4 bread slices on your work surface. Place one provolone cheese slice on the bread. Place 2 tomato slices on each sandwich over the cheese. Place the remaining cheese slices over the tomatoes. Place the remaining bread over the sandwiches.

Spread the mayonnaise over the outside slices of each sandwich. In a large skillet over medium heat, add the sandwiches. Cook for 3 minutes on each side or until golden brown. Remove the skillet from the heat and serve.

Grilled Pimento Cheese Sandwiches

Makes 8 sandwiches

1 1/4 cups mayonnaise
4 oz. jar diced red pimentos, drained
1 tsp. Worcestershire sauce
1 tsp. finely grated onion
4 cups shredded cheddar cheese
16 slices frozen Texas Toast garlic bread

In a mixing bowl, add the mayonnaise, red pimentos, Worcestershire sauce, onion and cheddar cheese. Stir until combined. Refrigerate the pimento cheese at least 2 hours before serving.

Preheat the oven to 400°. Place the garlic bread slices on two large baking pans. Bake for 5 minutes. Remove the garlic bread from the oven. The garlic bread will not be toasted at this point.

Spread the pimento cheese on one side of 8 garlic bread slices. Place the remaining bread slices over the pimento cheese. You will need to cook the sandwiches in batches. In a large skillet over medium heat, add the sandwiches. Cook for 3 minutes on each side or until the bread is toasted and the pimento cheese melts. Remove the sandwiches from the skillet and serve.

Pizza Grilled Cheese

Makes 1 serving

1 tbs. unsalted butter, softened
2 slices bread
1 oz. slice provolone cheese
6 pepperoni slices
3 tbs. pizza sauce

Spread the butter on one side of each bread slice. On one unbuttered side of a bread slice, place the provolone cheese. Place the pepperoni over the cheese. Spread the pizza sauce over the top. Place the remaining bread slice, buttered side up, over the sandwich.

In a skillet over medium heat, add the sandwich. Cook for 3 minutes on each side or until the cheese melts and the sandwich is golden brown. Remove from the heat and serve.

Bacon, Garlic & Onion Grilled Cheese

Makes 4 sandwiches

8 slices bacon, diced
1 onion, thinly sliced
8 slices frozen Texas Toast garlic bread
8 slices cheddar cheese, 1 oz. each

In a large skillet over medium heat, add the bacon. Cook for 10 minutes or until the bacon is crispy. Remove the bacon from the skillet and drain on paper towels. Add the onion to the skillet. Saute the onion for 5 minutes. Remove the skillet from the heat and drain off any excess grease from the onions.

Preheat the oven to 400°. Place the garlic bread slices on a baking sheet. Bake for 5 minutes. Remove the garlic bread from the oven. The garlic bread will not be toasted at this point.

Place 1 slice cheddar cheese over 4 garlic bread slices. Spoon the bacon and onions over the cheese. Place the remaining cheddar cheese slices over the bacon. Place the remaining bread slices over the cheese.

In a large skillet over medium heat, add the sandwiches. Cook for 3 minutes on each side or until the bread is toasted and the cheddar cheese melted. Remove the sandwiches from the skillet and serve.

Chicken Pepper Jack Grilled Cheese

Makes 4 servings

4 tbs. bottled peppercorn ranch salad dressing
8 rye bread slices
12 oz. thinly sliced cooked chicken breast
8 bacon slices, cooked
8 slices Pepper Jack cheese, 1 oz. size
2 tbs. unsalted butter, softened

Spread the peppercorn ranch dressing on one side of each bread slice. Place the chicken and bacon over the dressing on 4 slices. Place the Pepper Jack cheese over the top. Place the remaining bread slices over the sandwiches.

Spread the butter on the outside bread slices. In a large skillet over medium heat, add the sandwiches. Cook about 3 minutes on each side or until the cheese melts and the sandwiches are golden brown. Remove the skillet from the heat and serve.

Old Fashioned Grilled Cheese

Makes 4 servings

1/4 cup mayonnaise
8 bread slices
8 American cheese slices, 1 oz. size

Spread the mayonnaise on one side of each bread slice. In a large skillet over medium heat, add 4 bread slices with the mayonnaise side down. Place 2 American cheese slices over each piece of bread. Place the remaining bread, mayonnaise side up, over the sandwiches.

Cook for 3-4 minutes on each side or until the cheese is melted and the sandwiches are golden brown. Remove the skillet from the heat and serve.

Havarti Pork Grilled Cheese Sandwiches

Makes 4 servings

1/2 cup mango chutney
8 hearty bread slices
8 Havarti cheese slices, 1 oz. size
8 oz. thinly sliced cooked pork tenderloin
2 tbs. softened unsalted butter

Spread one side of each bread slice with the chutney. Place one Havarti cheese slice over the chutney on 4 bread slices. Place the pork tenderloin over the cheese. Place one cheese slice over the pork. Place the remaining bread, chutney side down, over the sandwiches.

Spread the butter on the outside bread slices. In a large skillet over medium heat, add the sandwiches. Cook about 3 minutes on each side or until golden brown. Remove from the heat and serve.

Havarti Swiss Grilled Cheese

Makes 6 servings

12 bread slices
6 Havarti cheese slices, 1 oz. size
6 Swiss cheese slices, 1 oz. size
3 tbs. unsalted butter, softened

Place one Havarti cheese slice and one Swiss cheese slice on 6 bread slices. Place the remaining bread slices over the cheese. Spread the butter on the outside bread slices.

In a large skillet or griddle over medium heat, add the sandwiches. Cook for 3 minutes on each side or until golden brown. Remove the skillet from the heat and serve.

Delicious with Pepper Gazpacho. This is one of our favorite soup and sandwich combination that we eat year round. The soup is so refreshing in the summer and the grilled cheese fills us up.

Apple Ham Grilled Cheese

Makes 4 servings

1 cup chopped apple
1/3 cup mayonnaise
1/4 cup finely chopped walnuts
8 slices Velveeta cheese, 1 oz. size
8 slices sourdough bread
8 slices fully cooked ham, 1 oz. size
1/4 cup unsalted butter, softened

In a small bowl, add the apple, mayonnaise and walnuts. Stir until combined. Place 1 slice Velveeta cheese on 4 bread slices. Spread the apple filling over the cheese. Place 2 ham slices over the cheese. Place 1 cheese slice on each sandwich over the ham. Place the remaining bread slices on the top.

Spread the butter on the outside slices of the sandwiches. In a large skillet or griddle over medium heat, add the sandwiches. Cook for 3 minutes on each side or until golden brown. Remove the skillet from the heat and serve.

Strawberry Goat Cheese Grilled Cheese

Makes 3 servings

4 oz. goat cheese log, softened
6 whole grain bread slices
4 1/2 tsp. red pepper jelly
3/4 cup sliced fresh strawberries
6 fresh basil leaves
1 1/2 cups arugula
Salt and black pepper to taste

Spread the goat cheese on one side of 3 bread slices. Spread the pepper jelly on one side of the remaining 3 bread slices. Place the strawberries, basil and arugula over the goat cheese slices. Season to taste with salt and black pepper. Place the remaining bread slices, pepper jelly side down, over the sandwiches.

Lightly spray a large skillet with non stick cooking spray and place the skillet over medium heat. Add the sandwiches to the skillet. Cook about 3 minutes on each side or until golden brown. Remove the skillet from the heat and serve.

Pepper Jack Grilled Cheese Sandwiches

Makes 6 servings

12 slices bread
3 tbs. softened unsalted butter
12 slices Pepper Jack cheese, 1 oz. size
2 cups fresh baby spinach
6 thin slices purple onion

Spread the butter on one side of each bread slice. Turn 6 bread slices over and place 2 slices Pepper Jack cheese on each piece of bread. Place about 1/3 cup spinach and 1 onion slice over the cheese on each sandwich. Place the remaining bread on the sandwiches with the butter side up.

On a large griddle over medium heat, add the sandwiches. Cook for 3 minutes on each side or until golden brown. Remove the sandwiches from the griddle and serve.

Perfect with Taco Vegetable Soup.

Monterey Jack Cheese Soup

Makes 5 servings

1 cup chicken broth
1 cup diced tomato
1/2 cup finely chopped onion
2 tbs. chopped green chiles
1 garlic clove, minced
2 tbs. unsalted butter
2 tbs. all purpose flour
3 cups whole milk
Salt and black pepper to taste
1 1/2 cups shredded Monterey Jack cheese

In a sauce pan over medium heat, add the chicken broth, tomato, onion, green chiles and garlic. Stir until combined and bring to a boil. Reduce the heat to low and place a lid on the pan. Simmer for 10 minutes. Remove the pan from the heat.

In a skillet over medium heat, add the butter. When the butter melts, add the all purpose flour. Stir constantly and cook for 2 minutes. Add 1 1/2 cups milk to the skillet. Stir constantly and cook until the sauce thickens and bubbles. Season to taste with salt and black pepper. Add the Monterey Jack cheese to the skillet. Stir until the cheese melts and remove the skillet from the heat. Stir in 1 1/2 cups milk.

Add the cheese sauce to the vegetables. Place the pan over medium heat. Stir constantly and cook about 3 minutes or until the soup is hot. Do not let the soup boil. Remove the pan from the heat and season to taste with salt and black pepper.

Egg Drop Soup

Makes 4 servings

3 cups chicken broth
1 tbs. cornstarch
2 tbs. cold water
1 egg, beaten
1 green onion, sliced

In a sauce pan over medium heat, add the chicken broth. Bring to a boil. In a small bowl, add the cornstarch and water. Whisk until combined and add to the broth. Stir constantly and bring to a boil. Stir constantly and cook for 2 minutes.

Drizzle the egg into the hot broth. Stir constantly and cook for 30 seconds. Remove the pan from the heat and stir in the green onion.

Cheddar Cheese Soup

Makes 8 cups

1/4 cup unsalted butter
1/2 cup finely chopped carrots
1/2 cup finely chopped celery
1/2 cup finely chopped green bell pepper
2 garlic cloves, minced
1/3 cup all purpose flour
1 chicken bouillon cube
2 cups whole milk
3 cups water
8 oz. cheddar cheese, freshly grated
1/4 tsp. cayenne pepper

In a dutch oven over medium heat, add the butter. When the butter melts, add the carrots, celery, green bell pepper and garlic. Saute for 7 minutes. Sprinkle the all purpose flour over the vegetables. Stir constantly for 2 minutes. Add the chicken bouillon cube, milk and water to the pan. Stir constantly and cook about 10 minutes or until the bouillon cube melts and the soup thickens and bubbles. Add the cheddar cheese and cayenne pepper to the pan. Stir constantly and cook until the cheese melts. Remove the pan from the heat and serve. Delicious served with Guacamole BLT.

Beer Cheese Soup

Makes 5 cups

1/4 cup unsalted butter
1/4 cup all purpose flour
2 cups half and half
12 oz. can beer
1 lb. Velveeta cheese, cubed
1 tbs. Worcestershire sauce
1/4 tsp. cayenne pepper
1/4 tsp. Tabasco sauce
1/8 tsp. salt
Black pepper to taste

In a dutch oven over medium heat, add the butter. When the butter melts, add the all purpose flour. Stir constantly and cook for 2 minutes. Add the half and half and beer to the pan. Stir constantly and cook about 5 minutes or until the soup is smooth and thickens.

Add the Velveeta cheese to the pan. Stir constantly and cook until the cheese melts. Add the Worcestershire sauce, cayenne pepper, Tabasco sauce and salt to the pan. Stir until combined and cook for 2 minutes. Remove the pan from the heat and season to taste with black pepper.

Cheese & Bacon Chowder

Makes 3 servings

6 bacon slices
1/4 cup chopped onion
2 tbs. all purpose flour
1/4 tsp. dry mustard
1/8 tsp. black pepper
1 tsp. Worcestershire sauce
3 cups whole milk
2 cups shredded cheddar cheese

In a large sauce pan over medium heat, add the bacon. Cook for 8 minutes or until the bacon is crisp. Remove the bacon from the pan and drain on paper towels. Drain off the bacon drippings.

Add the onion to the pan. Saute for 5 minutes. Add the all purpose flour, dry mustard, black pepper and Worcestershire sauce to the pan. Stir constantly and cook for 2 minutes.

Add the milk to the pan. Stir constantly and cook for 8 minutes or until the chowder begins to thicken. Remove the pan from the heat and cool for 10 minutes. Crumble the bacon and add to the pan. Add the cheese to the pan. Place the pan back on the stove over low heat. Stir constantly and cook only until the cheese melts and the soup is hot. Remove the pan from the heat and serve.

Cheese Vegetable Chowder

Makes 6 servings

1/4 cup unsalted butter
2 cups chopped cabbage
1 cup sliced onion
1 cup chopped celery
1 cup thinly sliced carrots
15 oz. can cream style corn
8 oz. can green peas, drained
2 1/2 cups whole milk
1/4 tsp. black pepper
1/2 tsp. dried thyme
2 1/2 cups shredded cheddar cheese

In a dutch oven over medium heat, add the butter. When the butter melts, add the cabbage, onion, celery and carrots. Saute for 8 minutes. Add the corn, green peas, milk, black pepper and thyme to the pan. Stir until combined and reduce the heat to low.

Stir occasionally and simmer for 20 minutes. Add the cheddar cheese to the pan. Stir until the cheese melts. Remove the pan from the heat and serve.

Cheese Tortellini Vegetable Soup

Makes 6 servings

5 cups chicken broth
3 1/2 cups shredded carrot
1 cup chopped yellow squash
3 cups torn fresh spinach
9 oz. pkg. refrigerated cheese tortellini

In a large sauce pan over medium heat, add the chicken broth, carrots and squash. Bring to a boil and reduce the heat to medium low. Simmer for 3 minutes. Add the spinach and tortellini to the pan.

Stir until combined and place a lid on the pan. Simmer for 5 minutes or until the tortellini is tender. Remove the pan from the heat and serve.

5 FISH & SEAFOOD SOUPS & SANDWICHES

Fish sandwiches are my personal favorite. I love Po Boys, fried fish and shrimp. Tuna is always a delicious stand by for sandwiches. Try the different variations and I am sure you will find one you love.

Shrimp Club Sandwich

Makes 4 servings

3 cups water
12 oz. fresh shrimp, peeled and deveined
8 oz. can pineapple tidbits, drained
1/2 cup chopped celery
2 tbs. finely chopped green onions
2 tbs. mayonnaise
8 slices sandwich bread, toasted and buttered
8 slices bacon, cooked crisp
8 tomato slices, about 1/4" thick
Salt and black pepper to season

Add the water to a large sauce pan and place the pan over medium heat. When the water is boiling, add the shrimp. Cook about 4 minutes or until the shrimp turn pink. Remove the pan from the heat and drain all the water from the shrimp. Rinse the shrimp in cold water until chilled. Drain all the water from the shrimp. Pat the shrimp dry with paper towels if needed.

Refrigerate the shrimp until well chilled. When the shrimp are chilled, chop the shrimp into small pieces. Place the shrimp in a mixing bowl and add the pineapple, celery, green onions and mayonnaise to the bowl. Stir until well combined.

Spread the shrimp filling on one side of 4 bread slices. Place 2 bacon slices and 2 tomato slices over the shrimp. Season to taste with salt and black pepper. Place the remaining bread slices over the top and serve.

Open Face Shrimp Sandwiches

Makes 4 servings

1/4 cup mayonnaise
2 tbs. prepared pesto
12 oz. cooked shrimp, peeled & deveined
6 French bread slices, toasted
1/3 cup shredded Parmesan cheese

In a mixing bowl, add the mayonnaise, pesto and shrimp. Stir until combined and spread on one side of each French bread slice. Place the sandwiches on a baking sheet. Sprinkle the Parmesan cheese over the top of the sandwiches.

Preheat the oven to 400°. Bake for 10 minutes. Remove from the oven and serve.

Delicious with Baked Potato Soup.

Shrimp Salad Croissants

Makes 8 servings

1 lb. cooked small shrimp, peeled & deveined
2 celery ribs, diced
1 cup shredded carrot
1 cup mayonnaise
1/3 cup finely chopped onion
1/8 tsp. salt
1/8 tsp. black pepper
4 oz. sliced almonds
8 croissants, split and toasted

In a mixing bowl, add the shrimp, celery, carrots, mayonnaise, onion, salt, black pepper and almonds. Stir until combined. Cover the bowl and refrigerate at least 2 hours before serving.

When ready to serve, spread the shrimp salad on the bottom of the croissants. Place the top on the sandwiches and serve.

Cajun Shrimp Sandwich

Makes 6 servings

1 cup unsalted butter
2 onions, chopped
1 1/2 tsp. minced garlic
1 tsp. Creole seasoning
3 lbs. fresh shrimp, peeled and deveined
16 oz. loaf frozen garlic bread, thawed

In a large dutch oven over medium heat, add the butter. When the butter melts, add the onions, garlic and Creole seasoning. Saute for 6 minutes or until the vegetables are tender. Add the shrimp and stir until combined. Place a lid on the pan and cook for 8 minutes or until the shrimp turn pink. Remove the pan from the heat.

While the shrimp are cooking, toast the bread. Separate the garlic bread into halves. Place the garlic bread on a baking sheet. Preheat the oven to 350°. Bake for 8 minutes or until the bread is toasted. Remove the bread from the oven and place on a serving platter. Spoon the shrimp over the garlic bread. Cut into slices and serve.

Shrimp Avocado Sandwiches

Makes 4 servings

4 bacon slices
1 lb. fresh shrimp, peeled and deveined
1/2 tsp. salt
1/4 tsp. black pepper
1/4 cup fresh lemon juice
1 1/2 cups cherry tomatoes, halved
5 oz. pkg. fresh arugula
1 cup fresh corn kernels
1/4 cup thinly sliced purple onion
1 tbs. olive oil
Salt and black pepper to taste
4 frozen Texas toast garlic bread slices
2 tbs. mayonnaise
2 avocados, peeled and sliced

In a skillet over medium heat, add the bacon. Cook for 8 minutes or until the bacon is crispy. Remove the bacon from the skillet and drain on paper towels. Add the shrimp to the skillet. Sprinkle 1/2 teaspoon salt over the shrimp. Cook for 4 minutes or until the shrimp turn pink. Remove the skillet from the heat. Add the black pepper and lemon juice to the skillet. Toss until the shrimp are coated in the lemon juice.

In a mixing bowl, add the cherry tomatoes, arugula, corn, purple onion and olive oil. Toss until combined. Season to taste with salt and black pepper.

Preheat the oven to 400°. Place the garlic bread slices on a baking sheet. Bake for 5 minutes or until the bread is toasted. Remove the garlic bread from the oven and place on a serving platter. Crumble the bacon.

Spread the mayonnaise over one side of the garlic bread. Place the bacon, shrimp and avocados over the mayonnaise. Spoon the arugula salad over the top and serve.

Garlic Tuna Melts

Makes 4 servings

12 oz. can albacore tuna, drained
4 tbs. finely chopped onion
4 tbs. finely chopped green bell pepper
2 tbs. finely chopped dill pickles
4 tbs. mayonnaise
8 slices frozen Texas Toast garlic bread, thawed
1/2 cup shredded cheddar cheese

In a mixing bowl, add the tuna, onion, green bell pepper, pickles and mayonnaise. Stir until combined. Preheat the oven to 400°. Place the garlic bread slices on a baking pan. Spread the tuna salad over 4 of the bread slices. Sprinkle the cheddar cheese over the top of the tuna. Place the remaining bread slices over the top.

Bake for 15 minutes or until the garlic bread is toasted and the cheese melted. Remove the sandwiches from the oven and serve.

Swiss Tuna Melts

Makes 4 servings

2 cans drained flaked tuna, 5 oz. size
3/4 cup shredded Swiss cheese
1/2 cup sour cream
1/2 cup mayonnaise
1/4 cup chopped onion
1/4 cup chopped celery
Black pepper to taste
8 bread slices
2 tbs. softened unsalted butter

In a mixing bowl, add the tuna, Swiss cheese, sour cream, mayonnaise, onion and celery. Stir until combined and season to taste with black pepper. Spread the tuna on one side of 4 bread slices. Place the remaining bread slices over the top. Spread the butter on the outside slices.

In a large skillet over medium heat, add the sandwiches. Cook about 3 minutes on each side or until golden brown. Remove the skillet from the heat and serve.

Delicious with Creamy Vegetable Soup and fruit salad.

Mediterranean Tuna Salad Sandwiches

Makes 4 sandwiches

1/4 cup mayonnaise
1/2 tsp. dried oregano
1 tbs. red wine vinegar
4 cans drained flaked tuna, 5 oz. size
2 tbs. sliced black olives
2 tbs. finely chopped red bell pepper
2 tbs. sliced green onions
4 lettuce leaves
4 French rolls, split and halved lengthwise

In a mixing bowl, add the mayonnaise, oregano and red wine vinegar. Stir until combined. Add the tuna, black olives, red bell pepper and green onions to the bowl. Stir until combined.

Place a lettuce leaf on the bottom of each roll. Spoon the tuna over the top. Place the top on the rolls and serve.

Tuna Burgers

Makes 6 burgers

1 egg, beaten
2 cans drained flaked tuna in water, 5 oz. size
1/2 cup crushed saltine crackers
1/4 cup finely chopped green bell pepper
2 tbs. finely chopped celery
2 tbs. finely chopped onion
1/4 tsp. black pepper
1 tsp. vegetable oil

In a mixing bowl, add the egg, tuna, crackers, green bell pepper, celery, onion and black pepper. Stir until combined and form into 6 patties.

In a large skillet over medium heat, add the vegetable oil. When the oil is hot, add the burgers. Cook for 4 minutes on each side or until golden brown. Remove the skillet from the heat and serve.

Veggie Tuna Burgers

Makes 6 burgers

1/4 cup finely chopped onion
1 garlic clove, minced
1 cup shredded zucchini
1 cup shredded yellow summer squash
1 cup shredded carrot
1 egg, beaten
2 cups soft breadcrumbs
5 oz. can flaked tuna, drained
1/4 tsp. salt
1/4 tsp. black pepper
1 tsp. unsalted butter

Spray a large skillet with non stick cooking spray. Place the skillet over medium heat. Add the onion and garlic to the skillet. Saute for 1 minute. Add the zucchini, yellow squash and carrot to the skillet. Saute for 4 minutes. Remove the skillet from the heat and cool completely before using.

In a mixing bowl, add the egg, breadcrumbs, tuna, salt and black pepper. Stir until combined. Add the vegetables to the bowl. Stir until combined. Form into 6 patties.

In a large skillet over medium heat, add the butter. When the butter melts, add the burgers. Cook for 4 minutes on each side or until golden brown. Remove the skillet from the heat. Serve the burgers with your favorite burger fixings if desired.

Herb Tuna Sandwiches

Makes 4 servings

12 oz. can flaked tuna, drained
2 hard boiled eggs, chopped
1/3 cup mayonnaise
1/4 cup minced chives
2 tsp. minced fresh parsley
1/2 tsp. dried basil
1/4 tsp. onion powder
8 slices bread, toasted
1/2 cup shredded cheddar cheese

In a mixing bowl, add the tuna, eggs, mayonnaise, chives, parsley, basil and onion powder. Stir until combined. Place 4 slices bread on a baking sheet. Spoon the tuna over the bread slices. Sprinkle the cheddar cheese over the top. Turn the oven to the broiler position. Broil for 2 minutes or until the cheese melts. Remove from the oven and place the remaining bread slices over the top. Serve immediately.

Tuna Cheese Sandwiches

Makes 5 servings

6 oz. pkg. flaked tuna, drained
1 cup shredded cheddar cheese
1/2 cup chopped walnuts
1/2 cup mayonnaise
1 tbs. whole milk
1 tsp. lemon juice
1/2 tsp. Worcestershire sauce
1/4 tsp. onion salt
1/8 tsp. black pepper
10 slices bread
2 1/2 cups finely shredded lettuce

In a mixing bowl, add the tuna, cheddar cheese, walnuts, mayonnaise, milk, lemon juice, Worcestershire sauce, onion salt and black pepper. Stir until combined and spread on one side of 5 bread slices. Sprinkle the lettuce over the top. Place the remaining bread slices over the sandwiches and serve.

Tuna Salad Sandwiches

Makes 6 servings

2 cans flaked & drained tuna, 5 oz. size
1/2 cup finely chopped celery
1 tsp. lemon juice
1/3 cup mayonnaise
2 tbs. sweet pickle relish
1/4 tsp. salt
1/8 tsp. black pepper
12 slices buttered toast
6 lettuce leaves
2 tomatoes, thinly sliced

In a mixing bowl, add the tuna, celery, lemon juice, mayonnaise, sweet pickle relish, salt and black pepper. Stir until combined and spread on one side of 6 toast slices. Place a lettuce leaf on each sandwich over the tuna salad. Place the tomatoes over the lettuce on each sandwich. Place the remaining toast slices over the top and serve.

Garlic Shrimp Po' Boys

Makes 4 servings

3 cups water
1 2 oz. fresh shrimp, peeled and deveined
2 tbs. finely chopped green onions
8 frozen Texas toast garlic slices, toasted
8 slices bacon, cooked crisp
8 tomato slices, about 1/4" thick
Salt and black pepper to season

Add the water to a large sauce pan over medium heat. When the water is boiling, add the shrimp. Cook about 4 minutes or until the shrimp turn pink. Remove the pan from the heat and drain all the water from the shrimp. Rinse the shrimp in cold water until they are chilled. Drain all the water from the shrimp. Pat the shrimp dry with paper towels if needed.

Refrigerate the shrimp until well chilled. When the shrimp are chilled, chop the shrimp into small pieces. Place the shrimp in a mixing bowl and add the green onions. Toss until well combined.

Spread the shrimp on one side of 4 garlic bread slices. Place 2 bacon slices and 2 tomato slices on each sandwich over the shrimp. Season to taste with salt and black pepper. Place the remaining garlic bread slices over the top and serve.

Curried Tuna Apple Sandwiches

Makes 6 sandwiches

1/2 cup mayonnaise
2 tbs. lemon juice
1 tsp. curry powder
1/4 tsp. garlic powder
12 oz. can albacore tuna, drained
1 large Granny Smith apple, chopped
2 celery ribs, chopped
1/2 cup raisins
4 tbs. diced onion
12 sandwich bread slices

In a mixing bowl, add the mayonnaise, lemon juice, curry powder and garlic powder. Stir until well combined and add the tuna, apple, celery, raisins and onion. Stir until well combined and spread on 6 bread slices. Top with the remaining bread slices and serve.

Grilled Salmon Sandwiches

Makes 4 servings

8 oz. can pink salmon, drained
1/3 cup finely chopped celery
1/4 cup mayonnaise
2 tbs. sweet pickle relish, drained
1/8 tsp. black pepper
8 slices Italian bread, 1/4" thick
1 egg
2/3 cup whole milk
1 tbs. unsalted butter

Remove the skin and bones from the salmon. Add the salmon to a mixing bowl along with the celery, mayonnaise, sweet pickle relish and black pepper. Stir until combined. Spread the salmon on one side of 4 bread slices. Place the remaining bread slices over the top.

In a small bowl, add the egg and milk. Whisk until combined. Dip each sandwich in the egg wash allowing the excess liquid to drip off back into the bowl. In a skillet over medium heat, add the butter. When the butter melts, add the sandwiches. Cook for 4 minutes on each side or until the sandwiches are golden brown. Remove the skillet from the heat and serve.

Grilled Fish Sandwiches

Makes 4 servings

4 green onions, minced
2 garlic cloves, minced
1/4 cup olive oil
1/4 cup dry white wine
2 tbs. lemon juice
1/2 tsp. salt
1 tsp. black pepper
4 grouper fillets, 5 oz. each & 1/2" thick
4 kaiser rolls, split
4 green lettuce leaves
1 large tomato, sliced
4 thin slices purple onion
1/4 cup tartar sauce

In a sauce pan over medium heat, add the green onions, garlic and olive oil. Saute for 4 minutes. Add the white wine, lemon juice, salt and black pepper to the pan. Saute for 1 minute. Remove the pan from the heat and cool completely before using.

Add the green onion marinade to a Ziploc bag. Add the grouper fillets to the bag. Close the bag and shake until the fillets are coated in the marinade. Refrigerate for 1 hour.

Have your grill hot and ready. Place the fillets over medium coals or 350°. Cook about 3-4 minutes on each side or until the fillets flake easily with a fork. Remove from the grill and place on the bottom half of the kaiser rolls. Place the lettuce, tomato and purple onion over the fillets. Spread the tartar sauce on the top half of the roll. Place over the sandwiches and serve.

Fried Grouper Sandwiches

Makes 4 servings

1/2 cup mayonnaise
1 tbs. chopped fresh basil
1 tbs. chopped fresh thyme
1 tbs. lemon juice
1 tsp. chopped fresh oregano
1 tsp. capers
1 garlic clove, minced
1 cup all purpose flour
1/4 cup cornstarch
1 tbs. garlic powder
3/4 tsp. black pepper
4 grouper fillets, 5 oz. each
1/2 tsp. salt
1/2 cup buttermilk
Vegetable oil for frying
4 onion sandwich buns, toasted
4 lettuce leaves
2 large tomatoes, sliced

In a small bowl, add the mayonnaise, basil, thyme, lemon juice, oregano, capers and garlic. Stir until combined. Cover the bowl and refrigerate for 2 hours before serving.

In a shallow dish, add the all purpose flour, cornstarch, garlic powder and 1/2 teaspoon black pepper. Stir until combined. Season the grouper fillets with 1/4 teaspoon black pepper and salt. Add the buttermilk to a small bowl.

In a dutch oven over medium heat, add vegetable oil to a depth of 3" in the skillet. The temperature of the oil should be 350° when ready. When the oil is hot, dredge the fillets in the seasoned flour. Dip the fillets in the buttermilk allowing the excess liquid to drip off back into the bowl. Dredge the fillets in the seasoned flour again.

Gently drop the fillets into the hot oil. Cook about 5 minutes or until the fillets are golden brown. Remove from the hot oil and drain on paper towels.

Spread the mayonnaise on the cut sides of the buns. Place a fillet on the bottom buns. Place the lettuce leaves and tomatoes over the fillets. Place the top on the sandwiches and serve.

Whitefish Reuben Sandwiches

Makes 4 sandwiches

1/2 cup whole milk
1/2 cup plain dry breadcrumbs
4 whitefish fillets, 5 oz. size
3 tbs. vegetable oil
2 tbs. unsalted butter
8 slices pumpernickel bread
4 Swiss cheese slices, 1 oz. size
3/4 cup sauerkraut
1/2 cup prepared Thousand Island dressing

Add the milk to a shallow bowl. Add the breadcrumbs to a shallow plate. Dip each fish fillet in the milk allowing the excess liquid to drip off back into the bowl. Dredge the fillets in the breadcrumbs.

In a skillet over medium high heat, add the vegetable oil. When the oil is hot, add the fish fillets. Cook for 3-4 minutes on each side or until the fillets flake easily with a fork. Remove the skillet from the heat.

Spread butter on one side of each bread slice. Place a Swiss cheese slice on the unbuttered side of 4 bread slices. Place the fillets over the cheese. Spoon sauerkraut over the fillets. Spread the Thousand Island dressing over the sauerkraut. Place the remaining bread slices, buttered side up, over the sandwiches.

In a large skillet over medium heat, add the sandwiches. Cook for 3 minutes on each side or until the cheese melts and the bread is toasted. Remove from the heat and serve.

Oyster Submarine Sandwich

Makes 8 servings

1 lb. loaf French bread
1 cup unsalted butter, softened
1/4 tsp. garlic salt
1 egg, beaten
2 tbs. water
1/2 cup dry breadcrumbs
2 large tomatoes, sliced 1/4" thick
8 bacon slices
1 pint oysters
2 tbs. all purpose flour
1/2 tsp. salt
1/8 tsp. black pepper
1 tsp. Worcestershire sauce
1 onion, thinly sliced
1 green bell pepper, cut into thin strips
2 tbs. unsalted butter, melted
1/4 cup mayonnaise
1/2 tsp. spicy mustard
1 lemon, cut into 8 wedges

Slice off the top third of the bread loaf. Remove the bread from the inside of the loaf leaving about a 1/2" shell around the loaf. Discard the removed bread or save for another recipe. In a small bowl, add 1/2 cup softened butter and 1/8 teaspoon garlic salt. Stir until combined and spread the butter on the inside of the bread.

Preheat the oven to 350°. Place the bread loaf on a baking sheet. Bake for 10-12 minutes or until the bread is lightly toasted. Remove the bread from the oven and set aside for now.

In a small bowl, add the egg and water. Stir until well combined. Place the breadcrumbs in a small shallow dish. Dip the tomato slices in the egg mixture allowing the excess egg to drip off back into the bowl. Dredge the tomato slices in the breadcrumbs. Place the tomatoes on a wire rack. Let the tomatoes sit for 30 minutes.

In a skillet over medium heat, add the bacon. Cook about 8 minutes or until the bacon is crispy. Remove the bacon from the skillet and drain on paper towels. Leave the bacon drippings in the skillet.

Add the tomatoes to the bacon drippings in the skillet. Fry about 3 minutes on each side or until the tomatoes are golden brown. Remove the tomatoes from the skillet and drain on paper towels.

Drain the oysters but reserve the liquid. You need 1 cup oyster liquid. If the oysters did not have 1 cup liquid, add water to make 1 cup. Add the oysters to the skillet and cook about 3 minutes. The edges of the oysters will curl when ready. Remove the skillet from the heat.

Oyster Submarine Sandwich cont'd

In a sauce pan over low heat, add 1/2 cup softened butter. When the butter melts, stir in the all purpose flour. Stir constantly and cook for 1 minute. The mixture should be smooth. Continue stirring and add the reserved oyster liquid. Cook until the sauce thickens and bubbles. Stir in the oysters, salt, black pepper, Worcestershire sauce and 1/8 teaspoon garlic salt.

Pour the oyster mixture into the hollowed out bread loaf. Place the fried tomato slices over the oyster mixture. Place the onion slices, green bell pepper and bacon over the top. Place the top slice of the bread loaf over the bread.

Preheat the oven to 400°. Brush 2 tablespoons melted butter over the outside of the loaf. Place the loaf back on the baking pan. Bake for 20 minutes or until the sandwich is thoroughly heated. Remove the bread from the oven. Cut the sandwich into 8 slices and spread the mayonnaise and mustard over the slices. Squeeze a lemon wedge over each slice before serving.

Crab Patties

Makes 4 servings

1 beaten egg
1/4 cup dry breadcrumbs
2 tbs. finely chopped onion
1 1/2 tsp. prepared horseradish
1 1/2 tsp. chopped red bell pepper
1 1/2 tsp. Dijon mustard
1/8 tsp. salt
1/8 tsp. cayenne pepper
1/4 cup mayonnaise
8 oz. cooked lump crabmeat
1 tbs. unsalted butter
2 English muffins, split and toasted
4 tomato slices
1/2 cup shredded Swiss cheese

In a mixing bowl, add the egg, breadcrumbs, onion, horseradish, red bell pepper, Dijon mustard, salt, cayenne pepper and mayonnaise. Stir until well combined. Add the crab to the bowl. Gently stir until combined. Form into 4 patties.

In a skillet over medium heat, add the butter. When the butter melts, add the crab patties. Cook for 3 minutes on each side or until golden brown. Remove the skillet from the heat.

Place the English muffins on a baking sheet. Place a crab patty over each muffin. Place the tomatoes over the patties. Sprinkle the Swiss cheese over the top. Turn the oven to the broiler position. Broil for 2 minutes or until the cheese melts. Remove from the oven and serve.

Fried Oyster Po' Boys

Makes 4 servings

1 lb. loaf French bread
1/4 cup unsalted butter, melted
1 1/3 cups self rising white cornmeal
2 containers drained oysters, 12 oz. size
6 cups vegetable oil
1/3 cup mayonnaise
2 1/2 tbs. sweet pickle relish
1 tbs. lemon juice
1/4 tsp. Tabasco sauce
1 cup shredded lettuce
1 large tomato, thinly sliced

Slice off the top 1/3 of the French bread loaf. Remove the bread from the bottom leaving about 1/2" shell on the bread. Save the removed bread for another use. Spread the butter on the inside of the bottom bread shell and the cut side of the top slice. Place the bread on a baking sheet.

Preheat the oven to 400°. Bake for 8 minutes or until the bread is hot and toasted. Remove from the oven. While the bread is baking, cook the oysters. In a mixing bowl, add the cornmeal. Add the drained oysters to the cornmeal. Toss until the oysters are coated in the cornmeal.

In a dutch oven over medium high heat, add the vegetable oil. The temperature of the oil should be 375°. When the oil is hot, add the oysters. Cook for 2-3 minutes or until the oysters are golden brown. Remove the oysters from the oil and drain on paper towels.

In a mixing bowl, add the mayonnaise, sweet pickle relish, lemon juice and Tabasco sauce. Stir until combined. Add the lettuce to the bowl. Toss until combined and spread in the bottom of the bread loaf. Spoon the oysters into the bread. Place the tomato slices over the top. Place the top of the bread on the sandwich and cut into 4 portions.

Spinach Oyster Sandwiches

Makes 4 servings

10 oz. pkg. frozen leaf spinach, thawed
1/2 cup sliced fresh mushrooms
2 1/2 tbs. plus 1 tsp. unsalted butter, softened
3 oz. pkg. cream cheese
1/8 tsp. salt
1/8 tsp. black pepper
4 slices French bread
1/8 tsp. garlic powder
16 large raw oysters
1/4 cup cream sherry
8 bacon slices, cooked and crumbled

In a large skillet over medium heat, add the spinach. Saute about 6 minutes or until the spinach is tender. Remove the skillet from the heat and drain all the liquid from the spinach. Remove the spinach from the skillet and set aside for now.

Add the mushrooms and 1 1/2 tablespoons butter to the skillet. Reduce the heat to low and cook for 6 minutes. Add the cream cheese, salt and black pepper. Stir until well combined and the cream cheese is melted. Add the spinach and stir until combined. Remove the skillet from the heat and keep the spinach warm while you prepare the rest of the dish.

Spread one side of each slice of bread with 1 teaspoon butter. Sprinkle the garlic powder over the butter. Set the bread aside for the moment.

Drain the oysters but reserve 1 tablespoon oyster liquid. Add 1 tablespoon oyster liquid and cream sherry to a skillet over medium heat. Add the oysters and cook for 8 minutes or until the oysters begin to curl. Remove the skillet from the heat.

Place the bread slices on a serving plate. Spoon the hot spinach mixture over the bread slices. Place 4 oysters on each bread slice. Place the bacon over the top and serve.

Open Face Crab Tomato Sandwiches

Makes 6 servings

2 large tomatoes
1 egg, beaten
3 oz. pkg. cream cheese, softened
1 tsp. lemon juice
2 tbs. chopped fresh parsley
2 tbs. grated Parmesan cheese
3 tbs. mayonnaise
1 cup cooked lump crabmeat
6 slices bread, crust removed

Slice each tomato into 3 slices. In a mixing bowl, add the egg, cream cheese, lemon juice, parsley, Parmesan cheese and mayonnaise. Stir until well combined. Gently stir in the crab meat.

Place the bread slices on a baking pan. Preheat the oven to 350°. Bake for 4 minutes or until the bread is lightly toasted. Remove the bread from the oven . Turn the oven to the broiler position. Place one tomato slice on one side of each bread slice. Spread the crab filling over the tomato slices. Broil for 2 minutes or until the sandwiches are hot and lightly browned. Remove the sandwiches from the oven and serve.

Crab Salad Croissants

Makes 4 servings

8 oz. cooked crabmeat, chopped
1/2 cup mayonnaise
1/4 cup chopped celery
2 tbs. shredded cheddar cheese
1 tbs. finely chopped onion
1 tsp. yellow prepared mustard
1/4 tsp. dried dill
1/8 tsp. salt
1/8 tsp. black pepper
4 lettuce leaves
4 croissants, split

In a small bowl, add the crabmeat, mayonnaise, celery, cheddar cheese, onion, mustard, dill, salt and black pepper. Stir until combined. Place a lettuce leaf on the bottom of the croissants. Spoon the salad over the lettuce. Place the top on the sandwiches and serve.

Open Face Crab Sandwiches

Makes 6 servings

1 lb. loaf French bread
1/4 cup unsalted butter, cubed
4 plum tomatoes, chopped
1 jalapeno pepper, seeded & chopped
2 garlic cloves, minced
2 tsp. minced fresh cilantro
1 lb. cooked lump crabmeat
3/4 cup ricotta cheese
1/2 cup sour cream
2 cups shredded Italian cheese blend

Cut the French bread loaf in half horizontally. Remove the bread from the top and bottom piece leaving about 1" shell on the loaves. Crumble the removed bread and place in a mixing bowl.

In a skillet over medium heat, add the butter. When the butter melts, add half the tomatoes, jalapeno pepper, garlic and cilantro. Stir until combined and cook for 4 minutes. Remove the skillet from the heat and spoon into the mixing bowl.

Add the crabmeat, ricotta cheese and sour cream to the bowl. Stir until combined and spread in the bread shells. Place the loaves on a baking sheet.

Sprinkle the Italian cheese blend over the top. Preheat the oven to 375°. Bake for 5-6 minutes or until the cheese melts. Remove from the oven and cut into slices to serve.

Seafood Salad Pitas

Makes 8 servings

2 cups chopped cooked crabmeat
1 cup chopped cooked shrimp
2 celery ribs, chopped
1/2 cup thinly sliced green onions
3/4 cup mayonnaise
3/4 tsp. seafood seasoning
1/4 tsp. salt
1/4 tsp. black pepper
4 pita bread rounds, 6" size

In a mixing bowl, add the crab, shrimp, celery, green onions, mayonnaise, seafood seasoning, salt and black pepper. Stir until combined. Cover the bowl and refrigerate at least 2 hours. Cut the pita bread rounds in half. Spoon the salad into the pitas and serve.

Oyster Corn Chowder

Makes 4 servings

2 cans drained whole oysters, 8 oz. size
14 oz. can cream style corn
1 cup half and half cream
2 cans drained sliced mushrooms, 4 oz. size
2 tbs. unsalted butter
1/4 tsp. Worcestershire sauce
1/8 tsp. black pepper

Add all the ingredients to a sauce pan over medium low heat. Stir constantly and cook about 6 minutes or until the chowder is thoroughly heated. Remove the pan from the heat and serve.

Salmon Corn Chowder

Makes 5 servings

1 tsp. vegetable oil
1/2 cup chopped onion
2 potatoes, peeled & cut into 1/2" pieces
15 oz. can cream style corn
1 1/2 cups water
1 1/2 cups evaporated milk
1/4 tsp. salt
7 oz. can salmon, drained and flaked
1/2 tsp. lemon pepper seasoning
1 tsp. dried dill

In a large sauce pan over medium heat, add the vegetable oil and onion. Saute for 4 minutes. Add the potatoes, cream style corn, water, evaporated milk and salt to the pan. Stir until combined and bring to a boil. Reduce the heat to low.

Simmer for 10 minutes or until the potatoes are tender. Add the salmon and lemon pepper to the pan. Stir until combined and cook for 10 minutes. Remove the pan from the heat and stir in the dill.

Halibut Chowder

Makes 8 servings

8 bacon slices
1/2 cup chopped onion
1 celery rib, chopped
4 cups chicken broth
4 red potatoes, cubed
2 tbs. all purpose flour
1 pint half and half cream
1 lb. halibut fillets, cubed
1 tsp. dried tarragon
1/2 tsp. salt
1/4 tsp. black pepper

In a sauce pan over medium heat, add the bacon. Cook about 7 minutes or until the bacon is crispy. Remove the bacon from the pan and drain on paper towels. Crumble the bacon. Drain all but 1 teaspoon drippings from the skillet.

Add the onion and celery to the pan. Saute for 4 minutes. Add the chicken broth and potatoes to the pan. Bring to a boil and reduce the heat to low. Simmer for 15 minutes or until the potatoes are tender.

In a small bowl, add the all purpose flour and half and half. Whisk until combined and add to the pan. Whisk constantly until the cream is smooth and combined. Add the halibut fillets, tarragon, salt and black pepper to the pan. Stir until combined.

Simmer for 10-12 minutes or until the halibut flakes easily with a fork. Remove the pan from the heat and serve.

Shrimp Vegetable Chowder

Makes 6 servings

1 1/2 tsp. instant chicken bouillon granules
2 cups hot water
4 bacon slices
1/3 cup chopped onion
1/3 cup unsalted butter
1/3 cup all purpose flour
1/2 tsp. salt
1/8 tsp. white pepper
3 cups whole milk
1 lb. pkg. frozen broccoli & cauliflower in cheese sauce
12 oz. frozen peeled & deveined shrimp

In a small bowl, add the chicken bouillon and water. Stir until the bouillon dissolves. In a dutch oven over medium heat, add the bacon. Cook for 8 minutes or until the bacon is crispy. Remove the bacon from the pan and drain on paper towels. Crumble the bacon.

Add the onion to the pan. Saute for 4 minutes. Add the butter to the pan. Stir until the butter melts. Add the all purpose flour, salt and white pepper to the pan. Stir constantly and cook for 2 minutes. Add the milk and chicken bouillon to the pan.

Stir constantly and cook about 6 minutes or until the chowder thickens. Add the broccoli & cauliflower with sauce to the pan. Add the frozen shrimp to the pan. Stir until well combined.

Stir frequently and cook about 10 minutes or until the vegetables and shrimp are tender. Remove the pan from the heat and serve.

Cajun Shrimp Soup

Makes 4 servings

1/2 cup chopped green bell pepper
1/4 cup sliced green onions
1 garlic clove, minced
1 tbs. unsalted butter
3 cups vegetable juice cocktail
8 oz. bottle clam juice
1/2 cup water
1/2 tsp. salt
1/4 tsp. crushed dried thyme
1/4 tsp. crushed dried red pepper flakes
1 bay leaf
1/3 cup dry long grain rice
12 oz. pkg. frozen peeled & deveined shrimp, cooked
Tabasco sauce to taste

In a large sauce pan over medium heat, add the green bell pepper, green onions, garlic and butter. Saute for 5 minutes. Add the vegetable juice cocktail, clam juice, water, salt, thyme, red pepper flakes, bay leaf and rice to the pan. Stir until combined.

Bring to a boil and reduce the heat to medium low. Place a lid on the pan. Simmer for 15 minutes or until the rice is tender. Add the shrimp to the pan. Stir until combined and cook for 3 minutes or until the shrimp are hot. Remove the pan from the heat. Remove the bay leaf and discard. Season to taste with Tabasco sauce.

6 MEATLESS SOUPS & SANDWICHES

I personally love meatless sandwiches and soups. These are some of my favorite meals. Every week, I fix at least 4 meatless meals for the family. We are trying to incorporate more plant based foods and less meat into our diet.

Living in the south, cold fruit or vegetable soups are perfect for an abundance of summer produce for hot days. If you are new to cold soups, start with fruit soups to adjust to the temperature and texture.

Vegetable Melt

Makes 4 sandwiches

1/4 cup mayonnaise
1 tbs. chopped fresh parsley
1/2 tsp. grated lemon zest
1 tbs. fresh lemon juice
8 bread slices
6 oz. pkg. sliced mozzarella cheese
1/4 cup chopped roasted red bell peppers
6 oz. jar marinated artichokes, drained & chopped
1 cup arugula
1/4 cup unsalted butter, softened

In a small bowl, add the mayonnaise, parsley, lemon zest and lemon juice. Stir until combined. Cover the bowl and refrigerate until chilled.

Spread the mayonnaise on one side of each bread slice. Place one mozzarella cheese slice on each sandwich over the mayonnaise on 4 bread slices. Spread 1 tablespoon red bell peppers, 1 tablespoon artichokes and 1/4 cup arugula on each sandwich over the cheese slice. Place the remaining cheese slices over the top of the sandwiches. Place the remaining bread slices, mayonnaise side down, over the sandwiches.

Spread the butter on the outside bread slices. In a large skillet over medium heat, add the sandwiches. Cook for 2-3 minutes on each side or until the cheese melts and the sandwiches are golden brown. Remove the skillet from the heat and serve.

Caribbean Quesadillas

Makes 6 servings

1 large sweet potato, peeled & diced
2 cups chopped onion
1 tsp. minced garlic
1 tsp. pumpkin pie spice
2 cans rinsed & drained black beans, 15 oz. size
1/2 cup chicken broth
12 flour tortillas, 8" size
1 1/2 cups shredded Monterey Jack cheese
4 oz. can diced green chiles
Sour cream & salsa to taste

Add the sweet potato to a microwavable bowl. Cover the bowl and microwave for 5 minutes or until the sweet potato is tender. Remove the bowl from the microwave.

In a large skillet over medium heat, add the onion, garlic and 1/2 teaspoon pumpkin pie spice. Saute for 5 minutes. Add the black beans and chicken broth to the skillet. Mash the beans slightly with a fork. Add the sweet potatoes to the skillet. Stir until combined. Taste the filling and season with the remaining pumpkin pie spice if desired. Cook about 5 minutes or until the filling is thoroughly heated. Remove the skillet from the heat.

Spread 3/4 cup bean filling on one side of 6 tortillas. Sprinkle 1/4 cup Monterey Jack cheese over the filling on each tortilla. Spoon 1 tablespoon green chiles over the filling on each tortilla. Place the remaining tortillas over the top.

You will need to cook the quesadillas in batches. In a large skillet over medium heat, add the quesadillas. Cook for 3 minutes on each side or until golden brown and the cheese melts. Remove from the skillet and serve with sour cream and salsa.

Bean Quesadillas

Use your favorite bean in this recipe if desired.

Makes 4 servings

15 oz. can red kidney beans, rinsed & drained
4 flour tortillas, 6" size
1/2 cup salsa
1/2 cup chopped yellow bell pepper
1 jalapeno pepper, seeded & chopped
1 garlic clove, minced
1 cup shredded Mexican cheese blend
1/8 tsp. Tabasco sauce
1 1/2 tsp. minced fresh cilantro

Preheat the oven to 350°. Add the beans to a small bowl. Mash the beans with a fork and spread on one side of 2 tortillas. Spread the salsa over the beans. Sprinkle the yellow bell pepper, jalapeno pepper, garlic and Mexican cheese blend over the top. Drizzle the Tabasco sauce over the filling. Sprinkle the cilantro over the filling.

Place the remaining tortillas over the quesadillas and place on a baking sheet. Bake for 10 minutes or until the cheese melts and the quesadillas are hot. Remove from the oven. Cut into wedges and serve.

Mushroom & Onion Reubens

Makes 4 sandwiches

2 cups sliced fresh mushrooms
1 cup thinly sliced onion, separated into rings
2 cups rinsed & drained sauerkraut
8 slices pumpernickel rye bread
4 slices Swiss cheese, 1 oz. size
3 tbs. sweet hot mustard

Spray a large skillet with non stick cooking spray. Place the skillet over medium heat. Add the mushrooms and onion to the skillet. Saute for 5 minutes or until the vegetables are tender. Reduce the heat to low. Add the sauerkraut to the skillet. Stir until combined. Stir occasionally and cook for 4 minutes. Remove the skillet from the heat.

Preheat the oven to the broiler position. Place the bread slices on a baking sheet. Broil for 1-2 minutes on each side or until the bread is toasted. Remove the bread from the oven. Place a Swiss cheese slice on 4 bread slices. Spread the mustard on one side of the remaining slices. Spoon the mushroom filling over the cheese. Place the top on the sandwiches and serve.

Garden Vegetable Quesadillas

Makes 4 quesadillas

1 tbs. olive oil
1 cup thinly sliced fresh mushrooms
1 onion, peeled & cut into thin wedges
1 red bell pepper, cut into thin strips
2 garlic cloves, minced
1/4 tsp. salt
1/4 tsp. black pepper
4 cups fresh baby spinach, cut into strips
1 tbs. chopped fresh cilantro
4 flour tortillas, 10" size
1 cup shredded mozzarella cheese
1 cup salsa

In a large skillet over medium heat, add the olive oil. When the oil is hot, add the mushrooms, onion, red bell pepper, garlic, salt and black pepper. Saute for 3 minutes. Add the spinach to the skillet. Saute for 2 minutes. Remove the skillet from the heat and stir in the cilantro.

Spoon the vegetables over one half of each tortilla. Sprinkle the mozzarella cheese over the top. Fold the tortilla over the filling. Preheat the oven to the broiler position. Place the quesadillas on a baking sheet. Broil for 2 minutes. Flip the quesadillas over and broil for 2 minutes. Remove from the oven and serve with the salsa.

Baked Eggplant Sandwiches

Makes 4 sandwiches

1 egg
1/4 cup Italian seasoned breadcrumbs
2 tbs. grated Parmesan cheese
4 eggplant slices, 3/4" thick & 4" in size
2 tbs. mayonnaise
2 tbs. Dijon mustard
4 kaiser rolls, split and toasted
1/4 cup sliced red onion, separated into rings
1 tomato, cut into 4 slices
4 lettuce leaves

Preheat the oven to 400°. Add the egg to a small bowl and beat until frothy. Add the breadcrumbs and Parmesan cheese to a small bowl. Stir until combined. Spray a baking sheet with non stick cooking spray. Dip each eggplant slice in the egg allowing the excess liquid to drip off back into the bowl. Dredge each eggplant slice in the breadcrumbs and place on the baking sheet.

Bake for 16-18 minutes or until the eggplant is tender and golden brown. Remove the pan from the oven. In a small bowl, add the mayonnaise and Dijon mustard. Stir until combined and spread on the cut sides of each roll. Place the eggplant slices on the bottom rolls.

Place the onion and tomato over the eggplant slices. Place a lettuce leaf on each sandwich. Place the top on the sandwiches and serve.

Antipasto Salad Hoagies

Makes 6 sandwiches

6 oz. jar marinated artichoke hearts
1 cup chopped fresh broccoli
1/4 cup chopped red onion
1 tsp. dried basil
6 cherry tomatoes, quartered
15 oz. can cannellini beans, rinsed & drained
2 tbs. white wine vinegar
6 unsliced hoagie buns, 6" size
1/2 cup shredded mozzarella cheese

Drain the artichokes but reserve the liquid in a small bowl. Chop the artichokes and add to a mixing bowl. Add the broccoli, onion, basil, tomatoes and cannellini beans to the bowl. Stir until combined.

Add the white wine vinegar to the artichoke liquid. Whisk until combined and pour over the salad. Toss until combined. Refrigerate for 20 minutes.

Cut 1/2" slice off the top of the hoagie buns. Remove the bread from the bottom pieces leaving about 1/2" shell on the buns. Spoon the salad into the bottom buns. Sprinkle the mozzarella cheese over the top. Place the top on the buns and serve.

Texas Toast Tomato Sandwiches

Makes 6 servings

6 slices frozen Texas toast garlic bread
6 tomatoes, sliced
Salt and black pepper to taste
1/3 cup bottled blue cheese vinaigrette dressing
6 tbs. chopped fresh basil
1/2 cup crumbled blue cheese

Preheat the oven to 375°. Place the garlic bread on a baking sheet. Bake for 8 minutes or until the garlic bread is toasted and golden brown. Remove the garlic bread from the oven.

Place the garlic bread on a serving platter. Place the tomato slices over the bread. Season to taste with salt and black pepper. Drizzle the blue cheese dressing over the tomatoes. Sprinkle the basil and blue cheese over the tomatoes and serve.

Mexican Fiesta Loaf

Makes 6 servings

1 lb. loaf round Italian bread
1/2 cup refried beans
4 oz. sliced Colby cheese
1 red bell pepper, sliced
4 oz. sliced mozzarella cheese
4 oz. can diced green chiles
1/2 cup sliced black olives
1 tomato, seeded and diced
1 cup shredded cheddar cheese
2 tbs. ranch salad dressing
1 avocado, peeled and sliced
4 slices cheddar cheese

Cut a 1" slice off the top of the bread loaf. Remove the bread from the inside of the loaf. Leave about a 1/2" shell on the loaf. Discard the removed bread or save for another recipe. Spread the refried beans inside the bread loaf. Place the Colby cheese, red bell pepper, mozzarella cheese, green chiles and black olives over the refried beans.

Gently press to combine the layers together. Place the tomato over the top of the sandwich layers. In a small bowl, stir together 1 cup shredded cheddar cheese and ranch dressing. Spread over the top of the tomato. Place the avocado slices over the top of the sandwich. Place the sliced cheddar cheese over the top. Place the top slice of bread on the sandwich. Cut into wedges and serve.

You can make the sandwich up to 4 hours before serving. Wrap in plastic wrap and refrigerate until ready to serve. I like to serve this sandwich hot for game day. I wrap the sandwich in aluminum foil and bake at 400° for 30 minutes or until the sandwich is warm.

Grilled Vegetable Sandwiches

Makes 4 servings

2 zucchini, cut into 1/2" slices
1 purple onion, cut into 1/4" slices
2 red bell peppers, cut into thin strips
1/4 cup plus 1 tbs. soy sauce
1/4 cup plus 1 tsp. lemon juice
1 tbs. honey
1/2 tsp. cayenne pepper
3 oz. goat cheese, softened
3 oz. pkg. cream cheese, softened
1 garlic clove, minced
1 tbs. crushed fresh rosemary
11" x 9" loaf focaccia bread

In a mixing bowl, add the zucchini, onion, red bell peppers, 1/4 cup soy sauce, 1/4 cup lemon juice, honey and cayenne pepper. Toss until combined and let the vegetables sit for 1 hour at room temperature. Stir occasionally while the vegetables are marinating.

In a small bowl, add the goat cheese, cream cheese, 1 tablespoon soy sauce, 1 teaspoon lemon juice, garlic and rosemary. Stir until combined and set aside for the moment.

Have your grill hot and ready. Spray your grill with non stick cooking spray. Place the vegetables on the grill. Grill the vegetables for 6 minutes or until they are tender. Remove the vegetables from the grill.

Trim 1/2" slice from the ends of the focaccia bread. Cut the bread into 4 equal squares. Slice each square horizontally in half. Spread the cut sides of the bread with the goat cheese spread. Place the vegetables on the bottom half of the bread squares. Place the top half on the sandwiches and serve.

Open Face Eggplant Sandwiches

Makes 8 servings

2 small eggplants, peeled
2 cups Italian seasoned breadcrumbs
3/4 cup grated Parmesan cheese
3 eggs
3 tbs. water
3 tbs. olive oil
2 French bread loaves, about 1 lb. each
2 cups spaghetti sauce
1 cup shredded mozzarella cheese

Slice the eggplants into 1/2" slices. In a shallow bowl, add the Italian breadcrumbs and Parmesan cheese. Stir until combined. Add the eggs and water to a shallow dish. Whisk until smooth and well combined.

Preheat the oven to the broiler position. Spray two baking sheets with non stick cooking spray. Dip each eggplant slice in the egg wash allowing the excess egg to drip off back into the bowl. Dredge each eggplant slice in the breadcrumbs. Place the eggplant slices on the baking sheets. Brush the olive oil over the eggplant slices. Broil about 5 minutes on each side or until the eggplant are tender. Remove the eggplant from the oven. Leave the broiler on.

Split the French bread loaves in half lengthwise. Place the bread halves, cut side up, on a baking sheet. Place the eggplant slices over the bread halves. Spread the spaghetti sauce over the eggplant. Sprinkle the mozzarella cheese over the sauce. Broil for 3 minutes or until the sauce is bubbly and the cheese melted. Remove from the oven. Cut into slices and serve.

Zesty Vegetable Wraps

Makes 4 servings

4 tbs. mayonnaise
2 tsp. lime juice
6 drops Tabasco sauce
4 spinach flour tortillas, 8" size
4 lettuce leaves
1 green bell pepper, julienned
4 slices Pepper Jack cheese

In a small bowl, add the mayonnaise, lime juice and Tabasco sauce. Stir until combined. Spread the mayonnaise on one side of each tortilla. Place the lettuce over the mayonnaise. Place the green bell pepper over the lettuce. Place a Pepper Jack cheese slice over the top. Tightly roll the sandwiches up and serve.

Grilled Open Faced Summer Sandwiches

Makes 4 servings

2 large tomatoes, cut into 1/2" slices
1 tsp. salt
1/2 tsp. black pepper
1/4 cup olive oil
4 French bread slices, about 1" thick
2 onions, cut into 1/2" slices
1/2 cup mayonnaise
3 tbs. prepared pesto
1 cup sliced black olives

Place the tomatoes slices on paper towels. Sprinkle the salt and black pepper over the tomatoes. Let the tomatoes sit for 5 minutes. Brush the olive oil over both sides of the bread slices. Place the French bread slices on a hot grill. Grill for 2 minutes on each side or until the bread is toasted. Add the onion slices to the grill and cook about 4 minutes on each side or until the onion slices are tender. Remove the bread and onions from the grill.

In a small bowl, add the mayonnaise and pesto. Stir until combined and spread on one side of each bread slice. Place the bread on a serving plate. Place the tomato and onion slices over the bread. Sprinkle the black olives over the top and serve.

Big Veggie Sandwiches

Makes 6 sandwiches

8 oz. container chive & onion cream cheese
12 slices whole wheat bread
6 green leaf lettuce leaves
1 green bell pepper, thinly sliced
1 large tomato, thinly sliced
2 avocados, peeled & sliced
1 cucumber, thinly sliced
3/4 cup alfalfa sprouts
1/3 cup Italian dressing

Spread the cream cheese on one side of each bread slice. Place the lettuce leaves, green bell pepper, tomato, avocados, cucumber and alfalfa sprouts over the cream cheese on 6 slices. Drizzle the Italian dressing over the vegetables. Place the remaining bread slices on the top and serve.

Vegetable Pita Sandwiches

Makes 4 servings

3 oz. cream cheese, softened
1 cup buttermilk
1 cup mayonnaise
1 cup sour cream
1 oz. pkg. dry ranch salad dressing mix
2 tbs. chopped fresh chives
2 tomatoes, chopped
1 cup chopped cucumber
1/2 cup chopped onion
2 carrots, shredded
2 pita rounds, cut in half
4 lettuce leaves
1/2 cup alfalfa sprouts

In a small bowl, add the cream cheese, buttermilk, mayonnaise, sour cream, ranch dressing mix and chives. Stir until well combined. In a mixing bowl, add the tomatoes, cucumber, onion and carrots. Stir until combined. Pour 1/2 cup dressing over the vegetables. Toss until combined. Place the lettuce leaves in the pita breads. Spoon the tomato filling into the pita breads. Sprinkle the alfalfa sprouts over the top. Drizzle with the remaining dressing and serve.

Veggie Pockets

Makes 6 servings

3 cups thinly sliced onion
2 tbs. vegetable oil
2 tbs. barbecue sauce
4 cups cooked broccoli florets
2 cups cooked cauliflower florets
1/4 cup mayonnaise
1/2 cup grated carrot
1/2 cup grated red cabbage
1/2 cup grated yellow squash
6 warm pita bread rounds, 6" size
2 cups shredded lettuce

In a skillet over medium heat, add the onion and vegetable oil. Saute for 8 minutes or until the onions begin to brown. Add the barbecue sauce, broccoli and cauliflower to the skillet. Stir until combined and cook about 4 minutes or until the vegetables are thoroughly heated. Remove the skillet from the heat. Add the mayonnaise, carrot, cabbage and squash to the skillet. Stir until combined. Cut each pita round in half. Sprinkle the pitas with lettuce. Spoon the vegetables into the pitas and serve.

Roasted Vegetable Sandwiches

Makes 4 servings

1 medium eggplant, peeled
1 tsp. salt
2 zucchini, cut into 1/4" thick slices
3 yellow squash, cut into 1/4" thick slices
1 red bell pepper, cut into 1/2" strips
1 onion, peeled and halved
3 tbs. olive oil
1/2 tsp. black pepper
3 tbs. chopped fresh basil
1 tbs. chopped fresh parsley
16 oz. loaf frozen garlic bread, thawed
4 provolone cheese slices

Cut the eggplant into 1/4" thick slices. Place the eggplant slices on paper towels. Sprinkle 1/2 teaspoon salt over the eggplant. Let the eggplant slices sit at room temperature for 20 minutes.

In a mixing bowl, add the eggplant, zucchini, yellow squash and red bell pepper. Cut the onion into 1/4" thick slices and add to the bowl. Sprinkle 1/2 teaspoon salt over the vegetables. Add the olive oil and black pepper to the bowl. Toss until the vegetables are coated in the olive oil.

Preheat the oven to 450°. Place the vegetables, in a single layer, on a large baking sheet. Bake for 20 minutes or until the vegetables are tender. Remove the vegetables from the oven and sprinkle the basil and parsley over the vegetables. Toss until combined.

Separate the garlic bread into halves. Place the vegetables on one garlic bread half. Place the provolone cheese slices over the top of the vegetables. Place the remaining garlic bread half over the top. Wrap the sandwich in aluminum foil. Bake for 30 minutes or until the garlic bread is toasted and the cheese melted. Remove the sandwich from the oven and serve.

Veggie Burgers

Makes 8 servings

1 cup dried lentils
2 1/2 cups water
1/4 cup ketchup
1/4 tsp. garlic powder
1/2 cup finely chopped onion
1 cup dry quick cooking oats
1 egg
1 tsp. salt
1/4 tsp. black pepper
1 tbs. whole wheat flour
2 tbs. vegetable oil

In a sauce pan over medium heat, add the lentils and water. Bring to a boil and reduce the heat to low. Place a lid on the pan and simmer for 25 minutes. Remove the lid from the pan. Simmer for 10 minutes or until the water is absorbed and the lentils are tender. Remove the pan from the heat.

Add the ketchup, garlic powder, onion, oats, egg, salt, black pepper and whole wheat flour to the pan. Stir until well combined. Form into 8 patties. In a skillet over medium heat, add the vegetable oil. When the oil is hot, add the burgers. Cook for 4 minutes on each side or until the burgers are golden brown. Remove the burgers from the skillet. Serve with your favorite burger fixings.

Grilled Garlic Vegetable Sandwiches

Makes 4 servings

2 zucchini, cut into 1/2" slices
1 purple onion, cut into 1/4" slices
2 red bell peppers, seeded and halved
3 oz. goat cheese, softened
3 oz. pkg. cream cheese, softened
1 garlic clove, minced
1 tbs. crushed fresh rosemary
8 slices Texas Toast frozen garlic bread, toasted

Have your indoor or outdoor grill hot and ready. Spray the grill with non stick cooking spray. Place the zucchini, purple onion and red bell peppers on the grill. Grill the vegetables for 6 minutes or until the vegetables are tender. Remove the vegetables from the grill.

In a small bowl, add the goat cheese, cream cheese, garlic and rosemary. Stir until combined. Spread the mixture on one side of the garlic bread slices. Place the vegetables over the cheese spread. Place the remaining bread slices over the vegetables and serve.

Goat Cheese Roasted Red Pepper Loaf

Makes 4 servings

16 oz. loaf French bread
8 oz. goat cheese, softened
2 jars drained roasted red bell peppers, 7 oz. size
12 large basil leaves
2 tsp. capers, drained
2 tbs. olive oil
1/4 tsp. salt
1/4 tsp. black pepper

Slice the bread horizontally in half lengthwise. Preheat the oven to 400°. Place the bread halves on a baking sheet. Bake for 5 minutes or until toasted. Remove from the oven.

Spread the goat cheese on the cut side of the bread halves. Place the red bell peppers on the bottom bread. Place the basil and capers over the peppers. Drizzle the olive oil over the top. Sprinkle the salt and black pepper over the sandwich. Place the top bread slice on the sandwich. Cut into 4 pieces and serve.

Three Cheese Tomato Melt

Makes 4 servings

8 slices frozen Texas toast garlic bread
1/2 cup shredded cheddar cheese
1/4 cup shredded mozzarella cheese
2 tbs. grated Parmesan cheese
4 tbs. mayonnaise
8 tomato slices, 1/2" thick

Preheat the oven to 400°. Place the garlic bread on a baking pan. Bake for 3 minutes. Remove the bread from the oven. In a small bowl, add the cheddar cheese, mozzarella cheese, Parmesan cheese and mayonnaise.

Place a tomato slice over each piece of garlic bread. Spread the cheese mixture over the top of the tomatoes. Bake for 5 minutes or until the garlic bread is toasted and the topping bubbly. Remove the sandwiches from the oven and serve.

Veggie Delight Sandwiches

Makes 4 servings

1/2 cup thinly sliced onion
2 cups sliced fresh mushrooms
1 tbs. unsalted butter
1/4 tsp. salt
1/4 tsp. black pepper
8 slices frozen Texas toast garlic bread
8 green bell pepper rings, 1/4" thick
4 slices colby jack cheese, 1 oz. each
8 thin tomato slices
24 thin zucchini slices
8 red bell pepper rings, 1/4" thick

In a skillet over medium heat, add the onion, mushrooms, butter, salt and black pepper. Saute the vegetables for 5 minutes. Remove the skillet from the heat. Preheat the oven to 400°. Place the garlic bread slices on a baking pan. Bake for 4 minutes. Remove the bread from the oven.

Spoon the mushroom filling over the garlic bread slices. Place a green bell pepper ring over each bread slice. Cut the colby jack cheese in half and place a slice over each piece of garlic bread. Place 1 tomato slice, 3 zucchini slices and 1 red bell pepper ring over each bread slice.

Turn the oven to the broiler position. Broil for 4 minutes or until the garlic bread is toasted and the vegetables lightly browned. Remove the sandwiches from the oven and serve.

Fried Green Tomato Sandwiches

Makes 8 servings

1 cup fine dry breadcrumbs
2 tbs. grated Parmesan cheese
1/2 tsp. salt
Pinch of cayenne pepper
2 eggs, beaten
4 large green tomatoes, cut into 1/4" slices
1/4 cup unsalted butter
1/3 cup ranch dressing
8 sandwich rolls, split
8 lettuce leaves
1 onion, thinly sliced
16 oz. pkg. bacon, cooked until crisp, optional

In a small bowl, add the breadcrumbs, Parmesan cheese, salt and cayenne pepper. Stir until well combined. Place the beaten eggs in a small bowl. Dip each tomato slice in the egg allowing the excess egg to drip off back into the bowl. Dredge each tomato slice in the breadcrumbs.

In a skillet over medium heat, add the butter. When the butter melts, add the tomato slices to the skillet. You will have to fry the tomatoes in batches. Cook the tomatoes about 3 minutes on each side or until they are golden brown. Remove the tomatoes from the skillet and drain on paper towels.

Spread the ranch dressing on one side of each roll. Place a lettuce leaf over the dressing. Place the onion slices and bacon slices over the lettuce. Place the green tomatoes over the bacon. Place the top over the filling and serve.

My family loves the bacon on this sandwich but I leave the bacon off my sandwich for a hearty tomato sandwich.

Fried Green Tomato Po' Boys

Makes 4 servings

1 cup mayonnaise
1/4 cup sliced green onion
2 tbs. Creole mustard
1 tbs. chopped fresh parsley
1 tbs. minced fresh garlic
1 tsp. prepared horseradish
1 beaten egg
1/2 cup buttermilk
1/2 cup self rising cornmeal
1/2 tsp. salt
1/2 tsp. black pepper
1/2 cup all purpose flour
3 firm green tomatoes, cut into 1/2" thick slices
Vegetable oil for frying
4 French baguettes, 6" size

In a small bowl, add the mayonnaise, green onion, Creole mustard, parsley, garlic and horseradish. Stir until combined. Cover the bowl and chill for 2 hours.

In a small bowl, add the egg and buttermilk. Whisk until well combined. In a shallow bowl, add the cornmeal, salt, black pepper and all purpose flour. Whisk until combined.

Dip each tomato slice in the egg wash allowing the excess liquid to drip off back into the bowl. Dredge each tomato slice in the seasoned flour making sure the tomatoes are covered in the flour.

In a 10" cast iron skillet over medium high heat, add vegetable oil to a depth of 1 1/2" inches in the skillet. The temperature of the oil should be 375°. You will need to fry the tomatoes in batches. If you add too many at one time to the oil, the temperature of the oil will drop and make the tomatoes greasy.

When the oil is hot, add the tomatoes. Cook about 2 minutes on each side or until golden brown. Remove the tomatoes from the skillet and drain on paper towels.

Cut each baguette in half lengthwise. Spread the sauce on the cut sides of the bread. Place the tomato slices over one side of the bread. Place the remaining bread slice over the top and serve.

Basil Red Pepper Sandwiches

Makes 4 servings

1 lb. loaf Italian bread
1 tsp. grated lemon zest
2 tbs. plus 1 tsp. olive oil
8 oz. sliced mozzarella cheese
1 cup jarred roasted red bell peppers, drained & patted dry
12 fresh basil leaves
1/2 cup chopped pimento stuffed olives

Cut the loaf of bread in half lengthwise. Remove the bread from the halves leaving about 1" shell on the loaves. Save the removed bread for another use.

In a small bowl, add the lemon zest and 2 tablespoons olive oil. Whisk until combined and brush on the cut side of the bread halves. Drizzle 1 teaspoon olive oil over the bottom bread loaf.

Place the mozzarella cheese in the bottom loaf. Place the red bell peppers, basil leaves and olives over the cheese. Place the top loaf on the sandwich. Cut into slices and serve.

Pear Waldorf Pitas

Makes 10 sandwiches

2 ripe pears, diced
1/2 cup thinly sliced celery
1/2 cup seedless red grapes, halved
2 tbs. finely chopped walnuts
2 tbs. lemon yogurt
2 tbs. mayonnaise
10 miniature pita pockets, halved
10 lettuce leaves

In a mixing bowl, add the pears, celery, grapes, walnuts, yogurt and mayonnaise. Stir until well combined. Cover the bowl and refrigerate for 1 hour.

Place the lettuce leaves inside the pitas. Remove the filling from the refrigerator and spoon about 2 tablespoons filling in each pita.

Spicy Minestrone

Makes 5 quarts

1/4 cup olive oil
1 1/3 cups chopped onion
1 1/3 cups chopped celery
1 cup sliced carrot
1 garlic clove, minced
3 cups chopped cabbage
1 1/2 cups frozen cut green beans
1 cup frozen whole kernel corn
1 cup frozen green peas
46 oz. bottle spicy hot V-8 juice
15 oz. can navy beans, drained
14 oz. can diced tomatoes
6 cups water
1 tbs. chopped fresh parsley
1 tsp. dried oregano
1/2 tsp. black pepper
1 tbs. Tabasco sauce
1/8 tsp. dried crushed red pepper flakes
2 cups dry elbow macaroni

In a large dutch oven over medium heat, add the olive oil. When the oil is hot, add the onion, celery, carrot, garlic and cabbage. Saute for 6 minutes. Add the green beans, corn, green peas, V-8 juice, navy beans, tomatoes with juice, water, parsley, oregano, black pepper, Tabasco sauce and red pepper flakes to the pan.

Stir until combined and bring to a boil. Reduce the heat to low and place a lid on the pan. Stir occasionally and simmer for 45 minutes. Add the elbow macaroni to the pan. Stir until combined. Simmer for 10 minutes or until the macaroni is tender. Remove the pan from the heat and serve.

Italian Tomato Soup

This is so easy and so delicious!

Makes 4 servings

28 oz. can Italian seasoned tomatoes
2 cans condensed tomato soup, 10.75 oz. size
4 cups chicken broth
Black pepper to taste

Add all the ingredients to a blender. Process until smooth and combined. In a large sauce pan over medium heat, add the soup. Stir constantly and cook about 6 minutes or until the soup is hot and bubbly. Remove the soup from the heat and season to taste with black pepper.

Cream Of Cabbage Soup

Makes 3 1/2 quarts

4 cups water
2 tbs. instant chicken bouillon granules
3 cups diced peeled potatoes
1 cup finely chopped onion
1 cup diced peeled rutabaga
1/2 cup diced carrots
6 cups chopped cabbage
1 cup chopped celery
1/2 cup chopped green bell pepper
1 garlic clove, minced
1 tsp. salt
1 tsp. dried dill
1 cup unsalted butter
1 cup all purpose flour
2 cups whole milk
2 cups chicken broth
8 oz. Velveeta cheese, cubed
1/2 tsp. dried thyme
Black pepper to taste

In a dutch oven over medium heat, add the water and chicken bouillon granules. Bring to a boil and add the potatoes, onion, rutabaga and carrots. Stir until combined and cook for 5 minutes.

Reduce the heat to medium low. Add the cabbage, celery, green bell pepper, garlic, salt and dill. Stir until combined and cook for 6 minutes or until the vegetables are tender.

While the vegetables are cooking, make the cheese sauce. In a skillet over medium heat, add the butter. When the butter melts, add the all purpose flour. Stir constantly and cook for 2 minutes. Add the milk and chicken broth to the skillet. Stir constantly and cook for 5 minutes or until the sauce thickens and bubbles. Add the Velveeta cheese and thyme to the skillet. Stir until the cheese melts. Remove the skillet from the heat and add to the vegetables.

Stir until combined and cook for 4 minutes. Remove the pan from the heat and season to taste with black pepper.

Tomato Soup With Herb Croutons

Makes 3 1/2 cups

1/2 cup chopped onion
4 tbs. melted unsalted butter
3 tbs. all purpose flour
1 cup chicken broth
28 oz. can Italian style tomatoes
3 tbs. tomato paste
1 tbs. minced fresh parsley
1 tbs. granulated sugar
1 tsp. salt
1 tsp. dried basil
1/4 tsp. black pepper
1 bay leaf
2 slices white bread
1 tbs. grated Parmesan cheese

In a dutch oven over medium heat, add the onion and 3 tablespoons butter. Saute for 4 minutes. Sprinkle the all purpose flour over the onion. Stir constantly and cook for 1 minute. Reduce the heat to low.

Add the chicken broth to the pan. Stir constantly and cook until the soup thickens and bubbles. Add the tomatoes with juice, tomato paste, parsley, granulated sugar, salt, 1/2 teaspoon basil, black pepper and bay leaf to the pan. Stir until combined and simmer for 30 minutes. Remove the bay leaf and discard. Remove the pan from the heat.

Using a hand blender, puree the soup. While the soup is cooking, make the croutons. Trim the crust from the bread slices. Brush 1 tablespoon melted butter over both sides of the bread. Sprinkle the Parmesan cheese and 1/2 teaspoon basil over the bread slices. Cut each bread slice into 4 squares. Cut each square into 2 triangles. Place the croutons on a baking sheet. Preheat the oven to 350°. Bake for 10 minutes or until the croutons are golden brown. Remove from the oven. Spoon the soup into bowls and sprinkle the croutons over the top.

Basil Tomato Soup

Makes about 1 gallon

2 cups chopped onion
4 tbs. olive oil
7 cans Italian seasoned diced tomatoes, 15 oz. size
4 cups chicken broth
1 cup fresh basil leaves
3 garlic cloves, peeled
1 tsp. grated lemon zest
1 tbs. lemon juice
1 tsp. salt
1 tsp. granulated sugar
1/2 tsp. black pepper
1/4 cup water

In a large dutch oven over medium heat, add the onions and 2 tablespoons olive oil. Saute for 8 minutes or until the onions are tender. Add the tomatoes and chicken broth to the pan. Stir until combined and bring the soup to a boil. Reduce the heat to low. Stir occasionally and simmer for 20 minutes.

Using a hand held blender, puree the soup. In a food processor, add the basil, garlic, lemon zest, lemon juice, salt, granulated sugar, black pepper, 2 tablespoons olive oil and water. Process until smooth and combined. Add to the soup. Stir until combined and cook for 2 minutes. Remove the pan from the heat and serve.

Fresh Tomato Soup

This is a delicious soup to make when the tomatoes and herbs are ripe in the garden.

Makes 4 servings

2 tsp. olive oil
4 garlic cloves, minced
8 cups diced fresh tomatoes
1/2 cup chopped green onions
1/2 cup chopped green bell pepper
2 tbs. granulated sugar
1 tsp. salt
1/4 cup chopped fresh cilantro

In a dutch oven over medium heat, add the olive oil and garlic. Saute for 2 minutes. Add the tomatoes, green onions, green bell peppers, granulated sugar and salt. Stir until combined and bring to a boil.

Reduce the heat to medium low. Place a lid on the pan and simmer for 8 minutes. Remove the pan from the heat and spoon the soup into bowls. Sprinkle the cilantro over the top and serve.

Yellow Tomato Soup With Goat Cheese Croutons

Makes 6 servings

9 medium yellow tomatoes, halved
3 tbs. olive oil
4 garlic cloves, minced
1 tsp. salt
2 tsp. black pepper
1 tsp. minced fresh rosemary
1 tsp. minced fresh thyme
1 1/4 cups chopped onion
1 cup vegetable broth
1/2 cup whole milk
1/2 cup heavy whipping cream
12 French baguette slices, 1/2" thick
2 tbs. prepared pesto
1/2 cup crumbled goat cheese

Preheat the oven to 400°. Spray a large baking sheet with non stick cooking spray. Place the tomatoes, cut side down, on the baking sheet. Brush 1 tablespoon olive oil over the tomatoes. Sprinkle 2 garlic cloves, salt, 1 teaspoon black pepper, rosemary and thyme over the tomatoes.

Bake for 25 minutes or until the tomatoes are tender and the skins charred. Remove from the oven and cool for 10 minutes. Remove the skins from the tomatoes and discard. Add the tomatoes to a blender and process until well blended.

In a sauce pan over medium heat, add the onion and 1 tablespoon olive oil. Saute for 5 minutes. Add 2 garlic cloves to the pan. Saute for 1 minute. Add the vegetable broth and milk to the pan. Stir until combined. Simmer for 15 minutes.

Add the whipping cream to the pan. Stir until combined and cook about 3 minutes or until the soup is thoroughly heated. Do not let the soup boil once you add the cream. Remove the pan from the heat and serve with the croutons.

While the soup is cooking, make the croutons. Preheat the oven to 400°. Place the baguette slices on a baking sheet. Brush the top of the croutons with 1 tablespoon olive oil. Bake for 5 minutes or until the croutons are golden brown.

Spread the pesto over the croutons. Sprinkle 1 teaspoon black pepper over the pesto. Sprinkle the goat cheese over the top. Bake for 2 minutes and remove from the oven.

Chunky Tomato Vegetable Soup

Makes 4 servings

10.75 oz. can condensed tomato soup
1 1/4 cups water
1 tomato, chopped
1 green bell pepper, chopped
1 zucchini, chopped
1/2 tsp. instant beef bouillon granules
1/2 tsp. crushed dried basil
1/4 tsp. Worcestershire sauce

In a sauce pan over medium heat, add all the ingredients. Stir until combined and bring to a low boil. Simmer for 5 minutes. Remove the pan from the heat and serve.

Cream Of Vegetable Soup

Makes 3 quarts

1 cup chopped onion
3/4 cup unsalted butter
1/2 cup all purpose flour
4 cups chicken broth
2 cups whole milk
2 cups half and half cream
1 tsp. dried basil
1/2 tsp. salt
1/2 tsp. black pepper
5 cups chopped cooked mixed vegetables

I use cooked fresh broccoli, cauliflower and carrots for the mixed vegetables. Use your favorite fresh or frozen vegetables in the soup. Leftover vegetables are wonderful in this soup.

In a dutch oven over medium heat, add the onion and butter. Saute for 5 minutes. Add the all purpose flour to the pan. Stir constantly and cook for 2 minutes. Add the chicken broth to the pan. Stir constantly and cook until the broth thickens and bubbles.

Add the milk, half and half, basil, salt, black pepper and vegetables to the pan. Stir constantly and cook about 4 minutes or until the soup is thoroughly heated. Do not let the soup boil once you add the milk. Remove the pan from the heat and serve.

Creamy Vegetable Soup

Makes 4 servings

2 cups chicken broth
1/4 cup diced carrot
1/4 cup diced celery
1/4 cup finely chopped onion
2 tbs. unsalted butter
1/4 cup all purpose flour
1/8 tsp. salt
2 cups whole milk
1/2 cup cubed Velveeta cheese

In a small sauce pan over medium heat, add the chicken broth. Bring the broth to a boil and add the carrot and celery. Saute for 5 minutes. Remove the pan from the heat.

In a large sauce pan over medium heat, add the onion and butter. Saute for 5 minutes. Sprinkle the all purpose flour and salt over the onion. Stir constantly and cook for 2 minutes. Add the milk to the pan. Stir constantly and cook about 3 minutes or until the soup thickens and bubbles.

Add the carrots and celery along with the Velveeta cheese to the soup. Stir constantly and cook until the cheese melts and the soup is thoroughly heated. Remove the pan from the heat and serve.

Delicious with Swiss Tuna Melts.

Roasted Root Vegetable Soup

Makes 16 cups

1 lb. parsnips, peeled & chopped
1 lb. turnips, peeled & chopped
1 lb. celeriac, peeled & chopped
2 lb. butternut squash, peeled & chopped
1/4 cup olive oil
10 cups chicken broth
1/4 cup unsalted butter
2 cups chopped onion
4 garlic cloves, minced
3 tbs. all purpose flour
3 tbs. tomato paste
2 tsp. Cajun seasoning
1 cup heavy whipping cream
1/2 tsp. salt

Preheat the oven to 450°. In a large bowl, add the parsnips, turnips, celeriac, butternut squash and olive oil. Toss until the vegetables are coated in the oil. Spread the vegetables in a large roasting pan in a single layer.

Bake for 1 hour or until the vegetables are tender and browned. Remove the pan from the oven. Add 6 cups chicken broth to the pan. Stir the broth and scrape the bottom of the pan to remove any food bits. Using a hand blender, puree until smooth.

In a large dutch oven over medium heat, add the butter. When the butter melts, add the onion and garlic. Saute for 7 minutes. Sprinkle the all purpose flour over the vegetables. Stir constantly and cook for 3 minutes or until the flour browns. Add the tomato paste and Cajun seasoning to the pan. Stir constantly and cook for 3 minutes. Add 4 cups chicken broth to the pan. Using a hand blender, process until the onions and garlic are pureed.

Add the vegetables and broth from the roasting pan to the dutch oven. Add the heavy cream and salt to the pan. Stir until combined and bring to a boil. Reduce the heat to low. Stir frequently and simmer for 15 minutes. Remove the pan from the heat and serve.

Ultimate Veggie Soup

This delicious soup is packed full of nutrition rich veggies.

Makes 6 servings

1 zucchini, chopped
1 1/3 cups chopped fresh mushrooms
1/2 cup chopped onion
4 garlic cloves, minced
1 tsp. canola oil
4 cups chicken broth
2 cans diced tomatoes with basil, oregano & garlic, 14 oz. size
1 lb. frozen chopped broccoli, thawed
2 carrots, shredded
1 cup meatless spaghetti sauce
1 tsp. dried Italian seasoning
1 tsp. adobo seasoning
10 oz. pkg. frozen chopped spinach, thawed and drained

Directions

In a dutch oven over medium heat, add the zucchini, mushrooms, onion, garlic and canola oil. Saute for 5 minutes. Add the chicken broth, tomatoes with juice, broccoli, carrots, spaghetti sauce, Italian seasoning and adobo seasoning. Stir until combined and bring to a boil.

Reduce the heat to low and place a lid on the pan. Simmer for 15 minutes or until the vegetables are tender. Add the spinach to the pan. Stir until combined and cook for 2 minutes. Remove the pan from the heat and serve.

Vegetarian Stew

Makes 5 servings

2 cups water
1 cup couscous
2 carrots, sliced
1 plum tomato, chopped
1/4 cup chopped onion
1 garlic clove, minced
2 cans tomato soup, 19 oz. size
15 oz. can black beans, rinsed & drained
10 oz. pkg. frozen chopped spinach, thawed & drained
1 tbs. minced fresh basil
1/2 tsp. salt
1/2 tsp. dried oregano
1/2 tsp. dried marjoram
1/4 tsp. black pepper
Shredded Parmesan cheese to taste

In a large sauce pan over medium heat, add the water. When the water is boiling, stir in the couscous, carrots, tomato, onion and garlic. Bring to a boil and reduce the heat to low. Stir occasionally and simmer for 10 minutes or until the couscous and vegetables are tender.

I use Progresso tomato soup in this recipe. You can use 2 cans condensed tomato soup with 2 cans water if desired. Add the tomato soups, black beans, spinach, basil, salt, oregano, marjoram and black pepper to the pan. Stir until combined and cook about 5 minutes or until the soup is hot and bubbly. Remove the pan from the heat and spoon into bowls. Sprinkle Parmesan cheese over the top and serve.

Roasted Vegetable Chili

Makes 5 quarts

2 lb. butternut squash, peeled & cut into 1" cubes
3 large carrots, sliced
2 zucchini, cut into 1" pieces
2 tbs. olive oil
1 1/2 tsp. ground cumin
2 green bell peppers, diced
1 1/4 cups chopped onion
3 cans chicken broth, 14 oz. size
3 cans diced tomatoes, 14 oz. size
2 cans rinsed & drained cannellini beans, 15 oz. size
1 cup water
1 cup salsa
3 tsp. chili powder
6 garlic cloves, minced

Preheat the oven to 450°. Place the butternut squash, carrots and zucchini on a large baking sheet. Drizzle 1 tablespoon olive oil over the vegetables. Sprinkle the cumin over the vegetables. Toss until the vegetables are coated in the oil and cumin. Bake for 25 minutes or until the vegetables are tender and golden brown. Remove from the oven.

While the vegetables are roasting, make the chili. In a dutch oven over medium heat, add the green bell peppers, onion and 1 tablespoon olive oil. Saute for 5 minutes. Add the chicken broth, tomatoes with juice, cannellini beans, water, salsa, chili powder and garlic to the pan. Stir until combined and bring to a boil. Reduce the heat to medium low. Stir occasionally and simmer for 10 minutes. Add the roasted vegetables to the pan. Stir until combined and cook for 10 minutes. Remove the pan from the heat and serve.

Meatless 5 Can Chili

This is too easy to make and you can have a hot supper in no time. Pair with your favorite sandwich for a quick and easy meal.

Makes 6 servings

15 oz. can chili with beans
15 oz. mixed vegetables, drained
11 oz. can Mexicorn, drained
10.75 oz. can condensed tomato soup
10 oz. can tomatoes with green chiles

Add all the ingredients to a sauce pan over medium heat. Stir until combined and bring to a boil. Stir constantly and cook for 4 minutes. Remove the pan from the heat and serve.

Weekday Vegetable Soup

Makes 7 cups

14 oz. can stewed tomatoes
1 cup tomato sauce
10 oz. pkg. frozen mixed vegetables
2 cups water
1 1/2 tsp. beef bouillon granules
1/8 tsp. black pepper

Add all the ingredients to a dutch oven over medium heat. Stir until well combined. Bring to a boil and reduce the heat to low. Place a lid on the pan. Stir occasionally and simmer for 20 minutes. Remove the pan from the heat and serve.

Add a grilled cheese or BLT to serve with the soup.

Cream Of Asparagus Soup

Makes 4 servings

1 cup chopped onion
1 garlic clove, minced
3 cups fresh trimmed asparagus, cut 1" pieces
2 1/2 cups chicken broth
1/8 tsp. crushed red pepper flakes
3 oz. cream cheese, cubed
2 tbs. sour cream
1 tbs. chopped fresh dill
1/2 tsp. ground nutmeg
Black pepper to taste

Spray a large non stick skillet with non stick cooking spray. Place the skillet over medium heat and add the onion and garlic. Saute for 5 minutes. Add the asparagus, chicken broth and red pepper flakes. Bring to a boil and reduce the heat to low. Place a lid on the skillet. Simmer for 10 minutes or until the asparagus is tender. Remove the skillet from the heat.

Spoon the vegetables and broth into a blender. Process until smooth. Pour the soup back into the skillet and place back on the stove over low heat. Add the cream cheese, sour cream, dill and nutmeg to the skillet. Stir constantly and cook only until the cream cheese melts and the soup is hot. Remove from the heat and season to taste with black pepper.

Corn And Zucchini Queso Chowder

Makes 11 cups

1/4 cup unsalted butter
1 cup finely chopped red bell pepper
1 cup finely chopped onion
3 poblano peppers, seeded & finely chopped
2 garlic cloves, minced
2 cups frozen whole kernel corn, thawed
2 cups chopped zucchini
1/4 tsp. ground cumin
2 cans chicken broth, 14 oz. size
1/3 cup all purpose flour
1 1/2 cups whole milk
1 cup half and half
1 cup freshly shredded Monterey Jack cheese
1 cup freshly shredded cheddar cheese
1/2 tsp. salt
1/2 cup diced purple onion

In a dutch oven over medium heat, add the butter. When the butter melts, add the red bell pepper, 1 cup finely chopped onion, poblano peppers and garlic. Saute for 7 minutes. Add the corn, zucchini and cumin to the pan. Saute for 7 minutes.

Add the chicken broth to the pan. Stir to remove any food bits stuck to the bottom of the pan. Bring to a boil and reduce the heat to low. Place a lid on the pan and simmer for 15 minutes.

In a small bowl, add the all purpose flour, milk and half and half. Whisk until combined and add to the pan. Stir constantly and cook about 5 minutes or until the chowder thickens.

Add the Monterey Jack cheese, cheddar cheese and salt to the pan. Stir until combined and the cheese melts. Remove the pan from the heat. Spoon into bowls and top with the purple onion.

Baked Potato Soup

This soup is made extra easy using frozen mashed potatoes.

Makes 8 cups

1/4 cup unsalted butter
1/2 cup chopped onion
1 garlic clove, minced
1/4 cup all purpose flour
1 chicken bouillon cube
3 cups water
24 oz. pkg. frozen mashed potatoes, thawed
2 cups whole milk
1/2 tsp. black pepper

In a dutch oven over medium heat, add the butter. When the butter melts, add the onion and garlic. Saute for 7 minutes. Sprinkle the all purpose flour over the vegetables. Stir constantly for 2 minutes.

Add the chicken bouillon cube and water to the pan. Stir constantly and cook about 10 minutes or until the bouillon cube melts and the soup thickens and bubbles. Add the mashed potatoes, milk and black pepper to the pan. Stir constantly and cook until hot. Remove the pan from the heat and serve.

Delicious with shrimp sandwiches.

Spinach Potato Soup

It is hard to believe how delicious this easy soup is to make.

Makes 4 servings

3 cups whole milk
15 oz. can sliced potatoes, drained
10 pkg. frozen creamed spinach, thawed
1/2 tsp. dried basil
1/2 tsp. garlic salt

Add all the ingredients to a large sauce pan over medium heat. Stir until combined and bring to a boil. Reduce the heat to low and place a lid on the pan. Stir occasionally and simmer for 15 minutes. Remove the pan from the heat. You can leave the soup chunky or puree the soup if desired.

Rustic Potato Soup

Makes 4 servings

3 cups water
5 cups russet potatoes, unpeeled & diced
2 cups whole milk
2 tsp. unsalted butter
1/2 tsp. salt
1/4 tsp. black pepper
1 cup sliced green onions
1 cup shredded sharp cheddar cheese

In a large sauce pan over medium heat, add the water. When the water is boiling, add the potatoes. Reduce the heat to medium low. Simmer for 10 minutes or until the potatoes are tender. Remove the pan from the heat and drain all the water from the potatoes.

Add 3 cups potatoes and 1 cup milk to a blender. Process until smooth and combined. Add the potatoes back to the pan. Add the remaining potatoes, 1 cup milk, butter, salt, black pepper, 3/4 cup green onions and 3/4 cup cheddar cheese to the pan.

Place the pan over medium heat. Stir constantly and cook about 6 minutes or until the soup is hot and the cheese melted. Remove the pan from the heat. Spoon the soup into bowls. Sprinkle the remaining green onions and cheddar cheese over the top.

Spinach Soup

Makes 6 servings

2 quarts water
2 envelopes dry vegetable soup mix(Knorr's)
10 oz. pkg. frozen chopped spinach
8 oz. can water chestnuts, drained & chopped
1/4 cup chopped green onions

Add all the ingredients to a sauce pan over medium heat. Stir until combined and bring to a boil. Reduce the heat to low. Stir frequently and cook for 15 minutes. Remove the pan from the heat and serve.

Broccoli Chowder

Makes 6 servings

4 cups fresh broccoli florets, chopped
2 potatoes, peeled & diced
1 1/2 cups water
2 carrots, thinly sliced
1 1/4 cups chopped onion
1 celery rib, finely chopped
4 cups whole milk
2 tsp. instant chicken bouillon granules
1 tsp. Worcestershire sauce
3/4 tsp. salt
1/2 tsp. black pepper
1/3 cup all purpose flour
1 cup Velveeta cheese, cubed

In a large sauce pan over medium heat, add the broccoli, potatoes, water, carrots, onion and celery. Bring to a boil and cook for 8 minutes or until the vegetables are tender.

Add 3 cups milk, chicken bouillon, Worcestershire sauce, salt and black pepper to the pan. Stir until combined. In a small bowl, add 1 cup milk and the all purpose flour. Whisk until combined and add to the soup. Whisk constantly and cook for 2 minutes or until the soup thickens. Remove the pan from the heat.

Add the Velveeta cheese to the soup. Stir until the cheese melts and serve.

Fiesta Soup

Makes 4 servings

2 cans diced tomatoes with green chiles, 10 oz. size
15 oz. can whole kernel corn, drained
15 oz. can black beans, rinsed & drained
Salt and black pepper to taste
1/2 cup shredded cheddar cheese

Add the tomatoes with juice, corn and black beans to a sauce pan over medium heat. Stir until combined and bring to a boil. Cook for 4 minutes. Remove the pan from the heat. Season to taste with salt and black pepper. Spoon the soup into bowls and sprinkle the cheddar cheese over the top.

You can season the soup with taco seasoning mix, chili powder or cumin if desired.

Refried Bean Soup

Makes 8 servings

28 oz. can crushed tomatoes
1/2 cup chopped onion
1/2 tsp. minced garlic
2 cans refried beans, 15 oz. size
1 tbs. minced fresh cilantro
5 corn tortillas, cut into 1/2" strips

In a large sauce pan over medium heat, add the tomatoes, onion and garlic. Stir until combined and bring to a boil. Reduce the heat to medium low. Simmer for 5 minutes.

Add the refried beans and cilantro to the pan. Stir until combined. Stir occasionally and simmer for 15 minutes. Remove the pan from the heat. While the soup is cooking, bake the tortillas.

Preheat the oven to 350°. Spread the tortilla strips on a baking sheet. Bake for 10 minutes or until crispy. Stir occasionally while baking. Remove from the oven. Spoon the soup into bowls and top with the tortilla strips.

Red Lentil Soup

Makes 10 cups

2 tbs. unsalted butter
1 cup diced onion
1 cup chopped carrots
1 cup chopped celery
4 garlic cloves, minced
28 oz. can diced tomatoes
2 cups dried red lentils
2 chicken bouillon cubes
5 cups water
1/2 tsp. ground cumin
1/2 tsp. salt
1/4 tsp. black pepper
1 cup chopped fresh basil

In a dutch oven over medium heat, add the butter. When the butter melts, add the onion, carrots, celery and garlic. Saute for 6 minutes. Add the tomatoes with juice, lentils, chicken bouillon cubes, water, cumin, salt and black pepper. Stir until combined and bring to a boil.

Stir occasionally and cook for 30 minutes or until the lentils are tender. Remove the pan from the heat and spoon into bowls. Sprinkle the basil over the top and serve. Delicious with Havarti Pork Grilled Cheese Sandwiches.

Hearty Lentil Soup

Makes 12 cups

8 cups beef broth
3 cups diced carrots
28 oz. can diced tomatoes
1 1/2 cups dried lentils, rinsed & sorted
1 cup dry brown rice
1 cup chopped onion
1/2 cup chopped celery
3 garlic cloves, minced
2 bay leaves
1/2 tsp. dried basil
1/2 tsp. dried oregano
1/4 tsp. dried thyme
1/2 cup chopped fresh parsley
2 tbs. balsamic vinegar
1 tsp. salt
1/2 tsp. black pepper

In a dutch oven over medium heat, add the beef broth. When the broth is boiling, add the carrots, tomatoes with juice, lentils, brown rice, onion, celery, garlic, bay leaves, basil, oregano and thyme. Stir until combined and bring to a boil. Reduce the heat to medium low.

Place a lid on the pan. Stir occasionally and simmer for 45 minutes or until the vegetables, lentils and rice are tender. Remove the pan from the heat. Remove the bay leaf and discard.

In a food processor, add the parsley, balsamic vinegar, salt and black pepper. Process until smooth and combined. Spoon the soup into bowls and drizzle the dressing over the top.

Spiced Butternut Soup

Makes about 1 gallon

2 tbs. unsalted butter
1 1/2 cups diced onion
1 1/2 cups diced red bell pepper
3 garlic cloves, minced
2 tbs. grated fresh ginger
2 lb. butternut squash, peeled & cubed
1 large sweet potato, peeled & cubed
1 large Granny Smith apple, peeled & cubed
4 cups chicken broth
2 bay leaves
1 tsp. curry powder
1/2 tsp. black pepper
3/4 cup whipping cream
1 tbs. fresh lime juice
Salt and black pepper to taste

In a large dutch oven over medium heat, add the butter, onion and red bell pepper. Saute for 8 minutes. Add the garlic and ginger to the pan. Saute for 2 minutes.

Add the butternut squash, sweet potato, apple, chicken broth, bay leaves, curry powder and 1/2 teaspoon black pepper. Stir until combined and bring to a boil. Reduce the heat to low and place a lid on the pan. Stir occasionally and simmer for 30 minutes or until the vegetables are tender. Remove the pan from the heat.

Using a hand blender, puree the soup. Add the whipping cream to the soup and stir until combined. Place the pan back on the stove over low heat. Cook only until the soup is thoroughly heated. Remove from the heat and stir in the lime juice. Season to taste with salt and black pepper.

Butternut Thyme Squash Soup

Makes 6 cups

3 lb. butternut squash
2 tbs. unsalted butter
1/4 cup chopped onion
4 fresh thyme sprigs
2 cups chicken broth
1 1/2 cups whole milk
1/2 tsp. salt
1/4 tsp. black pepper

Cut the squash in half lengthwise and remove the seeds and pulp. Preheat the oven to 400°. Spray a large baking sheet with non stick cooking spray. Place the squash, cut side up, on the baking sheet. Bake for 45 minutes or until the squash is tender. Remove from the oven and cool for 10 minutes.

In a dutch oven over medium heat, add the butter, onion and thyme. Saute for 5 minutes. Peel the squash and cut into cubes. Add to the pan. Add the chicken broth to the pan. Stir until combined and bring to a boil. Cook for 4 minutes.

Remove the thyme sprigs from the soup and discard. Remove the pan from the heat. Using a hand blender, puree the soup. Add the milk, salt and black pepper to the soup. Stir until combined and place the pan back on the stove. Cook only until the soup is thoroughly heated. Remove from the heat and serve.

Butternut Squash Soup

Makes 10 cups

2 carrots, cut into 1" pieces
1 cup chopped onion
3 tbs. olive oil
3 lb. butternut squash, peeled & cut into 1" pieces
6 cups chicken broth
1 tsp. grated orange zest
1 cup heavy cream
3 tbs. white wine vinegar
1 tbs. honey
3/4 tsp. salt
1/2 tsp. black pepper
1/2 tsp. Tabasco sauce

In a dutch oven over medium heat, add the carrots, onion and olive oil. Saute for 10 minutes or until the carrots are golden brown. Add the squash, chicken broth and orange zest to the pan. Stir until combined and bring to a boil. Reduce the heat to low. Place a lid on the pan.

Simmer for 25 minutes or until the squash is tender. Add the heavy cream, white wine vinegar, honey, salt, black pepper and Tabasco sauce to the pan. Stir until combined and remove the pan from the heat. Cool for 10 minutes. Using a hand blender, puree the soup. Serve hot.

Tomato Red Pepper Soup

Makes 4 servings

28 oz. can whole tomatoes
12 oz. jar roasted red bell peppers, drained
1/4 cup half and half
1 1/2 tsp. salt
1 tsp. granulated sugar
1/2 tsp. black pepper
2 garlic cloves, peeled

Add all the ingredients to a food processor. Process until smooth and combined. Pour the soup into a sauce pan over medium heat. Stir frequently and cook about 8 minutes or until the soup is hot and bubbly. Remove from the heat and serve.

This soup goes with most any sandwich but especially grilled cheese sandwiches.

Smoky Red Pepper Soup

Makes 8 cups

3 tbs. unsalted butter
6 large red bell peppers, chopped
1 1/2 cups diced onion
2 garlic cloves, minced
3 tbs. tomato paste
1 tbs. finely grated fresh ginger
2 tsp. smoked paprika
1 tsp. ground coriander
5 cups vegetable broth
2 bay leaves
1/4 cup whipping cream
Salt and black pepper to taste
2 tbs. prepared pesto

In a dutch oven over medium heat, add the butter. When the butter melts, add the red bell peppers and onion. Saute for 15 minutes. Add the garlic, tomato paste, ginger, paprika and coriander to the pan. Stir constantly for 2 minutes.

Add the vegetable broth and bay leaves to the pan. Stir until combined and bring to a boil. Reduce the heat to medium low. Stir frequently and cook for 20 minutes. Remove the bay leaves from the pan and discard.

Remove the pan from the heat. Using a hand blender, puree the soup. Add the whipping cream to the pan and stir until combined. Season to taste with salt and black pepper. Spoon the soup into bowls and spoon a dollop of pesto in the center of each bowl. Delicious with Pancetta Arugula Turkey Sandwiches.

Cheese Tortellini Tomato Soup

This is delicious with most any beef or chicken sandwich.

Makes 2 quarts

1 1/2 cups chopped onion
1 tbs. unsalted butter
2 lbs. plum tomatoes, quartered
3 cups vegetable broth
8 oz. can tomato sauce
1 tbs. minced fresh basil
1/4 tsp. salt
1/8 tsp. black pepper
4 cups water
1 cup dried cheese tortellini
1/3 cup shredded Parmesan cheese

In a dutch oven over medium heat, add the onion and butter. Saute for 6 minutes. Add the tomatoes, vegetable broth, tomato sauce, basil, salt and black pepper to the pan. Stir until combined and reduce the heat to low.

Simmer for 30 minutes. Remove the pan from the heat and cool for 10 minutes. While the soup is cooking, add the water to a sauce pan over medium heat. When the water is boiling, add the tortellini. Cook about 6 minutes or until the tortellini is tender. Remove the pan from the heat and drain all the water from the tortellini.

Using a hand blender, puree the soup. Add the tortellini to the soup. Place the pan back on the stove over medium heat. Stir constantly and cook about 3 minutes or until the soup is thoroughly heated. Remove the pan from the heat and spoon into bowls. Sprinkle the Parmesan cheese over the top and serve.

Cheese Tortellini Garden Soup

Makes 4 servings

2 tsp. olive oil
1 green bell pepper, chopped
2 cups eggplant, peeled & cut into 1/2" cubes
2 fresh tomatoes, chopped
2 cans beef broth, 14 oz. size
1/3 cup dry cheese tortellini
2 tbs. chopped fresh oregano
4 tsp. ketchup
1 zucchini, thinly sliced

In a dutch oven over medium heat, add the olive oil. When the oil is hot, add the green bell pepper and eggplant. Saute for 5 minutes. Add the tomatoes, beef broth, cheese tortellini, oregano and ketchup to the pan. Stir until combined and bring to a boil.

Reduce the heat to medium low and place a lid on the pan. Simmer for 5 minutes. Add the zucchini to the pan. Stir until combined. Simmer for 10 minutes or until the zucchini and tortellini are tender. Remove the pan from the heat and serve.

Roasted Red Pepper Soup

Try this soup instead of tomato soup with your sandwiches. You may never go back to tomato soup again.

Makes 6 servings

1 1/2 cups chopped onion
2 garlic cloves, minced
2 tsp. unsalted butter
2 jars drained roasted red bell peppers, 15 oz. size
2 cups vegetable broth
1/2 tsp. dried basil
1/4 tsp. salt
1 cup half and half cream

In a large sauce pan over medium heat, add the onion, garlic and butter. Saute for 5 minutes. Add the red bell peppers, vegetable broth, basil and salt to the pan. Stir until combined. Bring to a boil and reduce the heat to low.

Place a lid on the pan. Stir occasionally and simmer for 15 minutes. Remove the pan from the heat and cool for 10 minutes. Using a hand blender, puree the soup. Add the half and half cream and 1 cup pureed soup to a small bowl. Whisk until combined and add to the soup. Stir until combined.

Place the pan back on the stove over medium heat. Cook about 3 minutes or until the soup is thoroughly heated. Do not let the soup boil. Remove the pan from the heat and serve.

Roasted Yellow Pepper Soup

Makes 8 cups

6 large sweet yellow bell peppers
1 1/2 cups chopped onion
1 cup chopped leeks, white portion only
1/4 cup unsalted butter, cubed
2 cups peeled potatoes, cubed
5 cups chicken broth
1/2 tsp. salt
1/2 tsp. black pepper
Shredded Parmesan cheese, optional

Cut the yellow bell peppers in half. Remove the tops and seeds from the peppers. Place the peppers on a baking sheet. Turn the oven to the broiler position. Broil for 4 minutes or until the skins are blistered. Remove the peppers from the oven and add to a heat proof bowl. Cover the bowl with plastic wrap and let the peppers rest for 15 minutes. Remove the skins from the peppers.

While the peppers are cooling, add the onion, leeks and butter to a large sauce pan over medium heat. Saute for 5 minutes. Add the potatoes, chicken broth, salt and black pepper. Stir until combined and bring to a boil. Reduce the heat to medium low. Simmer for 30 minutes or until the potatoes are tender.

Finely chop the peppers and add to the pan. Stir until combined and remove the pan from the heat. Cool for 5 minutes. Using a hand blender, puree the soup. Spoon the soup into bowls and sprinkle the Parmesan cheese over the top.

Cream Of Broccoli Soup

Makes 9 cups

4 cups chicken broth
1 cup chopped carrot
1 celery stalk, chopped
1 cup chopped onion
1 baking potato, peeled & finely chopped
1 bay leaf
1 lb. broccoli florets
2 cups half and half
1/2 tsp. salt
1/8 tsp. black pepper

In a dutch oven over medium heat, add the chicken broth, carrot, celery, onion, potato and bay leaf. Bring to a boil and reduce the heat to medium low. Simmer for 25 minutes or until the vegetables are tender.

Add the broccoli to the pan. Place a lid on the pan and simmer for 10 minutes or until the broccoli is tender. Remove the bay leaf from pan and discard. Remove the pan from the heat.

Using a hand blender, puree the soup. Place the soup back on the heat. Add the half and half, salt and black pepper to the pan. Stir until combined and cook only until the soup is thoroughly heated. Do not let the soup boil once you add the half and half. Remove the pan from the heat and serve.

Rosemary Mushroom Soup

Makes 3 servings

1 cup sliced fresh mushrooms
2 garlic cloves, minced
1/4 cup unsalted butter
10.75 oz. can cream of mushroom soup
1 cup half and half cream
1 tsp. dried crushed rosemary
1/2 tsp. paprika
2 tbs. minced fresh chives

In a large sauce pan over medium heat, add the mushrooms, garlic and butter. Saute for 5 minutes or until the mushrooms are tender. Add the cream of mushroom soup, cream, rosemary and paprika. Stir constantly and cook only until the soup is hot. Do not let the soup boil.

Remove the pan from the heat and pour into bowls. Sprinkle the chives over the top and serve.

Cream Of Mushroom Soup

Pair this soup with a beef sandwich for a hearty meal.

Makes 10 cups

3 pkgs. sliced fresh mushrooms, 8 oz. size
1 cup finely chopped onion
3 tbs. melted unsalted butter
1/2 cup all purpose flour
2 cans chicken broth, 14 oz. size
3 cups whipping cream
1/4 cup dry white wine
1 1/2 tsp. salt
1 tsp. dried tarragon
1 tsp. Worcestershire sauce
1/4 tsp. black pepper

Chop the mushrooms. Remove the stems if desired. In a dutch oven over medium heat, add the mushrooms, onion and butter. Saute for 10 minutes or until the mushrooms are tender. Sprinkle the all purpose flour over the mushrooms. Stir constantly and cook for 2 minutes.

Add the chicken broth, whipping cream, wine, salt, tarragon, Worcestershire sauce and black pepper to the pan. Stir until combined and bring to a boil. Stir frequently and simmer for 20 minutes or until the soup thickens. Remove the pan from the heat and serve.

Mushroom Bisque

Makes 4 servings

8 oz. fresh mushrooms, sliced
1 cup sliced onion
1 cup minced fresh parsley
1/4 cup unsalted butter
1 tbs. all purpose flour
14 oz. can beef broth
1 cup sour cream

In a large sauce pan over medium heat, add the mushrooms, onion, parsley and butter. Saute for 8 minutes. Sprinkle the all purpose flour over the vegetables. Stir constantly and cook for 1 minute.

Add the beef broth to the pan. Stir constantly and cook about 4 minutes or until the soup thickens and bubbles. Using a hand blender, puree the soup. Add the sour cream to the soup. Stir until combined and remove the pan from the heat.

Portobello Ratatouille

Makes 10 servings

4 tbs. olive oil
2 large onions, peeled & sliced
4 garlic cloves, minced
12 oz. portobello mushrooms, gills removed & cubed
2 large eggplants, peeled & cubed
4 cups zucchini, cut into chunks
1/4 cup chopped fresh basil
1 tsp. salt
1 tsp. dried thyme
1/2 tsp. black pepper
28 oz. can diced tomatoes

In a dutch oven over medium heat, add 2 tablespoons olive oil. When the oil is hot, add the onions. Saute for 4 minutes. Add the garlic to the pan. Saute for 2 minutes. Add the mushrooms to the pan. Saute for 5 minutes. Remove the vegetables from the pan using a slotted spoon and drain on paper towels.

Add 2 tablespoons olive oil to the pan. When the oil is hot, add the eggplant and zucchini. Saute for 6 minutes. Add the basil, salt, thyme, black pepper and tomatoes with juice to the pan. Stir until combined and bring to a boil. Remove the pan from the heat. Add the mushrooms and onions to the pan. Stir until combined.

Preheat the oven to 350°. Place a lid on the pan. Bake for 45 minutes. Remove the lid from the pan. Bake for 45 minutes. Remove the pan from the oven and serve.

Speedy Tortilla Soup

Makes 4 servings

2 cans chicken broth, 14 oz. size
2 cups chopped fresh tomatoes
1/4 cup canned chopped green chiles
Salt and black pepper to taste
16 tortilla chips
1 cup shredded Monterey Jack cheese

In a sauce pan over medium heat, add the chicken broth, tomatoes and green chiles. Stir until combined and bring to a boil. Reduce the heat to low and place a lid on the pan. Simmer for 8 minutes. Remove the pan from the heat and season with salt and black pepper.

Place 4 tortilla chips in 4 bowls. Sprinkle the Monterey Jack cheese over the chips. Spoon the soup over the top and serve.

Mushroom Barley Soup

Makes 8 servings

8 cups beef broth
1/2 cup barley
3/4 tsp. sage
1/2 tsp. salt
1/4 tsp. garlic powder
2 tbs. unsalted butter
1/2 cup chopped onion
1/2 cup chopped green bell pepper
4 oz. jar sliced mushrooms, drained

In a dutch oven over medium heat, add the beef broth, barley, sage, salt and garlic powder. Stir until combined and bring to a boil. Reduce the heat to low and place a lid on the pan. Simmer for 45 minutes or until the barley is tender.

In a skillet over medium heat, add the butter, onion and green bell pepper. Saute for 5 minutes. Add the mushrooms to the skillet. Saute for 2 minutes. Remove the skillet from the heat and add to the soup. Stir until combined. Simmer for 15 minutes. Remove the pan from the heat and serve.

Southwestern Soup

This is one of our easiest and favorite soups. Serve with grilled cheese sandwiches for a hearty and comforting meal.

Makes 12 servings

3 cups water
4 cans tomato sauce, 8 oz. size
2 cans rinsed & drained red kidney beans, 15 oz. size
2 cans chicken broth, 14 oz. size
2 cups frozen whole kernel corn
2 cups salsa
2 tsp. dried minced onion
1 tsp. dried oregano
1 tsp. dried basil
2 cups shredded cheddar cheese

In a dutch oven over medium heat, add the water, tomato sauce, kidney beans, chicken broth, corn, salsa, dried onion, oregano and basil. Stir until combined and bring to a boil. Reduce the heat to medium low. Stir occasionally and simmer for 15 minutes. Remove the pan from the heat and spoon into bowls. Sprinkle the cheddar cheese over the top and serve.

Black Bean Soup

Makes 7 cups

1 lb. dried black beans
3 cans chicken broth, 14 oz. size
2 cups chopped onion
1 tbs. minced garlic
2 tbs. vegetable oil
10 oz. can diced tomatoes with green chiles
1/2 cup lemon juice
1/2 tsp. black pepper
1 tsp. Tabasco sauce
1 cup sour cream

Sort and rinse the black beans. Add the beans to a dutch oven over medium high heat. Add water to about 2" above the beans. Bring the beans to a boil and cook for 2 minutes. Remove the pan from the heat and place a lid on the pan. Let the beans rest for 1 hour.

Drain any water from the beans and place the beans on the stove over medium heat. Add the chicken broth to the beans. Bring to a boil and reduce the heat to medium low. Partially cover the beans with a lid. Simmer for 3 hours or until the beans are tender. Stir the beans occasionally while cooking. Remove the pan from the heat.

In a skillet over medium high heat, add the onion, garlic and vegetable oil. Saute for 5 minutes. Add the tomatoes with juice, lemon juice, black pepper and Tabasco sauce to the skillet. Saute for 4 minutes and remove the skillet from the heat. Add to a blender along with 2 cups black beans. Process until smooth and combined.

Add the puree to the pan with the remaining beans. Stir until combined and place the soup back on the stove over medium heat. Cook only until thoroughly heated. Remove from the heat. Spoon the soup into bowls and spoon a dollop of sour cream over each serving.

Cream Of Roasted Garlic Soup

This soup is delicious with chicken and beef sandwiches.

Makes 3 cups

2 large heads garlic
1 tbs. olive oil
1/2 cup finely chopped shallots
2 tbs. unsalted butter, melted
1 1/2 cups whole milk
1 cup whipping cream
1/2 cup cooked red potato, chopped
1/2 tsp. salt
1/2 tsp. minced fresh thyme
Black pepper to taste
Croutons, optional

Cut the tops off the garlic heads. Make sure to cut off enough so all the garlic cloves are exposed. Place each garlic head on a square of aluminum foil. Drizzle the olive oil over the top of the garlic heads. Wrap the foil around the garlic and place on a baking sheet.

Preheat the oven to 350°. Bake for 1 hour. Remove from the oven and cool completely. Squeeze the garlic cloves into a small bowl. In a sauce pan over medium heat, add the shallots and butter. Saute for 5 minutes. Add the milk, whipping cream and potato. Stir until combined and bring to a boil. Reduce the heat to low and simmer for 5 minutes. Remove the pan from the heat. Cool for 15 minutes.

Add the garlic to the sauce pan. Add the garlic cloves to the soup. Using a hand blender, puree the soup. Place the pan back on the heat. Add the salt and thyme to the pan. Stir constantly and cook only until the soup is thoroughly heated. Remove the pan from the heat and season to taste with black pepper. Spoon into bowls and sprinkle croutons over the top if desired.

Pumpkin Soup With Red Pepper Relish

Makes 10 cups

3 tbs. unsalted butter
5 carrots, chopped
1 1/4 cups chopped onion
2 garlic cloves, minced
5 cups chicken broth
1 tsp. salt
1/2 tsp. ground cumin
1/4 tsp. black pepper
2 cans pumpkin, 15 oz. size
1/4 cup whipping cream
12 oz. jar roasted red bell peppers, drained & finely chopped
2 tbs. chopped fresh cilantro
1 tbs. olive oil
1 tsp. fresh lime juice
1/4 tsp. smoked paprika

In a large dutch oven over medium heat, add the butter. When the butter melts, add the carrots, onion and garlic. Saute for 10 minutes. Add the chicken broth, 3/4 teaspoon salt, cumin and black pepper to the pan. Stir until combined and bring to a boil. Add the pumpkin to the pan. Stir until combined.

Reduce the heat to medium low. Simmer for 10 minutes. Remove the pan from the heat. Using a hand blender, puree the soup. Add the whipping cream to the soup and stir until combined.

In a small bowl, add the roasted red bell peppers, cilantro, 1/4 teaspoon salt, olive oil, lime juice and paprika. Stir until combined. Spoon the soup into bowls. Spoon the relish in the center and serve.

Pepper Gazpacho

Makes 8 cups

46 oz. bottle V-8 vegetable juice
12 oz. jar roasted red bell peppers, drained
1 cup fresh parsley leaves
1/2 cup chopped fresh basil leaves
1 1/2 cups chopped cucumber
1/2 cup jarred banana pepper rings
2 garlic cloves, minced
3 tbs. lemon juice
2 tbs. olive oil

In a blender, add half the V-8 juice, roasted red bell peppers, parsley, basil, 1 cup cucumber, banana pepper, garlic and lemon juice. Process until smooth and combined. Pour the soup into a serving bowl.

Add the remaining V-8 juice and olive oil to the bowl. Stir until combined. Cover the bowl and refrigerate about 2 hours or until chilled. When ready to serve, spoon the soup into bowls. Sprinkle 1/2 cup cucumber over the top and serve.

Delicious with Havarti Swiss Grilled Cheese.

Spanish Gazpacho

Makes 12 servings

5 lbs. fresh tomatoes, peeled & quartered
3 carrots, quartered
1 large cucumber, peeled & quartered
1 large red bell pepper, quartered
1 large green bell pepper, quartered
1 large onion, peeled & quartered
2 garlic cloves, minced
1/3 cup olive oil
3 tbs. balsamic vinegar
1 1/2 tsp. salt
1/2 tsp. black pepper

Unless you have a large blender, you will need to process the soup in batches. Add all the ingredients to a blender. Process until smooth and combined. Pour into a large serving bowl. Cover the bowl and refrigerate for 2 hours before serving.

Creamy Cucumber Soup

Being in the south, we love cold soups in the dog days of summer. Pair this soup with a sandwich that features ham or bacon for an easy supper on hot days.

Makes 4 cups

2 cucumbers, peeled, seeded & chopped
1 green onion, chopped
1 tbs. lemon juice
1 cup half and half
2 cups sour cream
1 tbs. minced fresh dill
1/2 tsp. salt
1/4 tsp. ground white pepper
Dash of Tabasco sauce

Add the cucumbers, green onion and lemon juice to a blender. Process until smooth and combined. Spoon into a bowl. Add the half and half, sour cream, dill, salt, white pepper and Tabasco sauce. Stir until combined.

Cover the bowl and refrigerate at least 3 hours before serving. Stir the soup again before serving.

Cream Of Carrot Soup

Makes 4 servings

4 cups chicken broth
4 cups carrots, cut into chunks
1/2 cup heavy whipping cream
1 tsp. granulated sugar

Add the chicken broth and carrots to a large sauce pan over medium heat. Bring to a boil and reduce the heat to medium low. Place a lid on the pan. Simmer for 15 minutes or until the carrots are tender. Remove the pan from the heat and cool for 10 minutes.

Using a hand blender, puree the carrots. Add the heavy whipping cream and granulated sugar to the pan. Stir until combined. Place the pan back on the stove over medium heat. Stir constantly and cook only until the soup is thoroughly heated. Do not let the soup boil once you add the cream. Remove the pan from the heat and serve.

Chilled Carrot Soup

Makes 5 cups

3 cups peeled & diced potatoes
2 cups diced carrots
1 1/2 cups chopped leeks
4 cups chicken broth
1 tbs. jarred chicken soup base
1 cup half and half
1/2 tsp. salt
1/4 tsp. ground white pepper

In a dutch oven over medium heat, add the potatoes, carrots, leeks, chicken broth and chicken soup base. Bring to a boil and reduce the heat to low. Place a lid on the pan and simmer for 10 minutes or until the vegetables are tender. Remove the pan from the heat and cool for 15 minutes.

Using a hand blender, puree the soup. Pour the soup into a large bowl. Add the half and half, salt and white pepper. Stir until combined. Refrigerate at least 4 hours but no longer than 24 hours before serving.

This is delicious with most any sandwich or grilled cheese.

Tomato Basil Bisque

If you love grilled cheese and tomato soup, this is the soup for you!

Makes 7 cups

2 cans condensed tomato soup, 10.75 oz. size
14 oz. can fire roasted diced tomatoes
2 1/2 cups whole milk
2 tbs. chopped fresh basil
1/4 tsp. black pepper
Shredded Parmesan cheese to taste

In a sauce pan over medium heat, add the tomato soup, tomatoes with juice, milk, basil and black pepper. Stir constantly and cook about 5 minutes or until the soup is thoroughly heated. Do not let the soup boil. Remove the pan from the heat.

Spoon the soup into bowls and sprinkle the Parmesan cheese over the top. Serve with your favorite grilled cheese.

Leek Soup

Makes 6 servings

6 thinly sliced leeks, white portion only
8 oz. pkg. fresh sliced mushrooms
1 garlic clove, minced
1/2 tsp. dried tarragon
1/4 tsp. white pepper
2 tbs. unsalted butter
7 1/2 tsp. all purpose flour
4 cups chicken broth
1/2 cup heavy whipping cream

In a dutch oven over medium heat, add the leeks, mushrooms, garlic, tarragon, white pepper and butter. Saute for 8 minutes or until the vegetables are tender. Sprinkle the all purpose flour over the vegetables. Stir constantly and cook for 2 minutes.

Add the chicken broth and whipping cream to the pan. Stir constantly and cook about 3 minutes or until the soup thickens and bubbles. Remove the pan from the heat and serve.

This is delicious with most any sandwich but I serve it with a Brie or American grilled cheese.

Weekday Cauliflower Soup

This is so easy but so good! Really filling on a cold day!

Makes 8 servings

1 head cauliflower, broken into florets
2 cans cream of chicken soup, 10.75 size
10.75 oz. can condensed cheddar cheese soup
14 oz. can chicken broth
2 cups whole milk

Add the cauliflower to a large sauce pan over medium heat. Cover the cauliflower with water. Bring to a boil and reduce the heat to medium low. Simmer for 6-8 minutes or until the cauliflower is crisp tender. Remove the pan from the heat and drain all the water from the pan.

In a large sauce pan over medium heat, add the cream of chicken soup, cheddar cheese soup, chicken broth and milk. Stir constantly and cook about 5 minutes or until the soup is hot. Add the cauliflower to the pan. Stir until combined and cook for 1 minute. Remove the pan from the heat and serve.

Ramen Corn Chowder

Makes 4 servings

2 cups water
3 oz. pkg. chicken ramen noodles
15 oz. can whole kernel corn, drained
15 oz. can cream style corn
1 cup whole milk
1 tsp. dried minced onion
1/4 tsp. curry powder
3/4 cup shredded cheddar cheese
1 tbs. crumbled cooked bacon
1 tbs. minced fresh parsley

In a sauce pan over medium heat, add the water. Bring the water to a boil and add the ramen noodles and seasoning packet. Reduce the heat to medium low and place a lid on the pan. Cook for 3 minutes or until the noodles are tender.

Add the whole kernel corn, cream style corn, milk, dried onion and curry powder to the pan. Stir until combined. Cook about 5 minutes or until the chowder is thoroughly heated. Do not let the chowder boil once you add the milk. Remove the pan from the heat and stir in the cheddar cheese, bacon and parsley. Spoon into bowls and serve. Great with most any chicken or turkey sandwich.

Corn Chowder

Makes 3 servings

10 oz. pkg. frozen cream style corn
3 bacon slices
1/4 cup chopped onion
1/4 cup chopped green bell pepper
3 tbs. all purpose flour
1/2 tsp. salt
1/8 tsp. black pepper
2 cups whole milk

Place the unopened package of corn in a large bowl of warm water. Let the corn sit for 20 minutes. In a skillet over medium heat, add the bacon. Cook for 8 minutes or until the bacon is crisp. Remove the bacon from the skillet and drain on paper towels. Crumble the bacon.

Add the onion and green bell pepper to the skillet. Saute for 5 minutes. Add the all purpose flour, salt and black pepper to the skillet. Stir constantly and cook for 2 minutes. Add the milk to the skillet. Stir constantly and cook about 5 minutes or until the chowder thickens. Add the corn to the skillet. Stir constantly and cook for 4 minutes. Remove the skillet from the heat. Spoon into bowls and sprinkle the bacon over the top.

Chilled Red Pepper Soup

Makes 8 servings

1 tbs. unsalted butter
3 cups chopped red bell pepper
1 cup chopped onion
1 garlic clove, minced
1 cup chicken broth
1/2 tsp. dried thyme
1/8 tsp. Tabasco sauce
1 cup half and half

In a large skillet over medium heat, add the butter, red bell pepper, onion and garlic. Saute for 5 minutes. Add the chicken broth, thyme and Tabasco sauce. Stir until combined and bring to a boil. Reduce the heat to low. Simmer for 12 minutes. Remove the pan from the heat.

Cool the soup for 5 minutes. Using a hand blender, puree the soup. Add the half and half cream to the soup. Stir until combined and spoon into a serving bowl. Cover the bowl and refrigerate for 4 hours before serving.

Chilled Berry Soup

This is so good with a chicken sandwich.

Makes 5 cups

2 pkgs. thawed frozen raspberries, 10 oz. size
2 cups dry red wine
2 1/2 cups water
3" stick cinnamon
1/4 cup granulated sugar
2 tbs. cornstarch
1/3 cup whipping cream

In a sauce pan over medium heat, add the raspberries, red wine, water, cinnamon and granulated sugar. Stir constantly and bring to a boil. Reduce the heat to low and simmer for 15 minutes. Remove the pan from the heat.

Strain the soup pressing the raspberry seeds from the soup. Pour the drained soup back into the sauce pan. Remove 1/4 cup soup from the pan and add to a small bowl. Add the cornstarch to the small bowl. Whisk until combined and add to the soup. Place the pan back on the stove over low heat. Stir constantly and cook until the soup begins to thicken. Remove the soup from the heat. Pour the soup into a serving bowl. Cover the bowl and refrigerate for 8 hours. When ready to serve, drizzle the whipping cream over the soup.

Strawberry Soup

Makes 2 servings

1 pint fresh strawberries, hulled
1/2 cup apple juice
1/2 cup granulated sugar
2 tbs. lemon juice
1 tsp. grated lemon zest

Add all the ingredients to a blender. Process until smooth and combined. Pour the soup into a bowl. Cover the bowl and refrigerate for 2 hours before serving.

Cold Peach Soup

Serve with chicken, fish or turkey sandwiches.

Makes 8 cups

1 1/2 lbs. peeled, sliced fresh peaches
1 cup sour cream
1 cup peach yogurt
1 1/2 cups orange juice
1 cup pineapple juice
1 tbs. fresh lemon juice
2 tbs. granulated sugar

Add the peaches, sour cream and yogurt to a food processor. Process until smooth and combined. Add the orange juice, pineapple juice and lemon juice to the food processor. Process until smooth and combined.

Pour the soup through a fine mesh strainer lined with cheesecloth into a serving bowl. Add the granulated sugar to the soup. Stir until the sugar dissolves. Cover the bowl and refrigerate at least 2 hours before serving. Stir the soup before serving.

Chilled Melon Soup

Makes 6 servings

3/4 cup orange juice
1 cup plain yogurt
1 cantaloupe, peeled, seeded & cubed
1 tbs. honey
1/4 tsp. salt
1/4 tsp. ground nutmeg
1/8 tsp. cayenne pepper
6 mint sprigs

In a blender, add the orange juice, yogurt and cantaloupe. Process until blended and pureed. Add the honey, salt, nutmeg and cayenne pepper. Process until combined.

Spoon the soup into a serving bowl. Cover the bowl and refrigerate at least 1 hour before serving. When ready to serve, spoon into bowls. Garnish each bowl with a mint sprig.

Chilled Cantaloupe Soup

Makes 6 servings

1 cantaloupe, seeded, peeled and cubed
2 cups orange juice
1 tbs. lime juice
1/2 tsp. ground cinnamon

In a large blender or food processor, add the cantaloupe and 1 1/2 cups orange juice. Process until smooth and combined. Pour the soup into a bowl. Add 1/2 cup orange juice, lime juice and 1/4 teaspoon cinnamon. Stir until combined. Cover the bowl and refrigerate for 2 hours before serving.

When ready to serve, sprinkle 1/4 teaspoon cinnamon over the top.

Chilled Fruit Soup

Makes 6 servings

15 oz. can sliced pears
10 oz. pkg. frozen sweetened raspberries, thawed
6 oz. can frozen orange juice concentrate, thawed
2 ripe bananas, peeled and cut into chunks
1/4 cup lemon juice
2 tsp. grated orange zest
1/2 cup sour cream
2 tbs. powdered sugar

In a blender, add the pears with juice, raspberries with any juice, orange juice concentrate, bananas, lemon juice and orange zest. Process until smooth and combined. Spoon into a large bowl. Cover the bowl and refrigerate for 2 hours.

When ready to serve, add the sour cream and powdered sugar to a small bowl. Stir until combined. Spoon the soup into bowls. Spoon a dollop of sour cream over the top.

Cold Peach Strawberry Soup

Makes 5 servings

1 fresh peach, peeled, pitted and sliced
1 cup sliced strawberries
8 oz. carton strawberry or peach yogurt
1 tbs. granulated sugar, optional
2 tbs. lemon juice
5 lemon slices
5 mint sprigs

In a blender, add the peach, strawberries, yogurt, granulated sugar and lemon juice. Process until smooth and combined. Spoon into a bowl. Cover the bowl and refrigerate for 2 hours or until well chilled.

When ready to serve, spoon the soup into bowls. Place a lemon slice and mint sprig for garnish over the soup.

CHAPTER INDEX

Beef Soup & Sandwiches

Grilled Garlic Steak Sandwiches, 2
Steak Stroganoff Sandwiches, 3
Giant Meatball Sandwich, 4
Pizza Meatball Subs, 5
Meatloaf Sandwiches, 6
Beef Stuffed Sourdough Sandwiches, 7
Cheeseburger Meatloaf Hoagies, 8
Basil Tomato Meatloaf Sandwiches, 9
Marinated Steak Sandwiches, 10
Stromboli Sandwiches, 11
Caramelized Onion Beef Sandwiches, 12
Cheese Steak Melts, 13
Cheesy Roast Beef Buns, 13
Horseradish Roast Beef Sandwiches, 14
Roast Beef BLT, 14
Hot Beef Sandwiches With Au Jus, 15
Round Steak Sandwiches, 15
Salt Roasted Beef Tenderloin Sliders With Chimichurri Pesto, 16
Spicy Shredded Beef Sandwiches, 17
Smothered Beef Sandwiches, 17
Cheddar French Dip Sandwiches, 18
Beef Stroganoff Sandwiches, 19
Garlic Sloppy Joes, 20
Ground Beef Reuben Melts, 21
Spicy Coleslaw Reubens, 21
Grilled Reubens With Homemade Dressing, 22
Garlic Bread Meatball Sandwiches, 23
French Beef Sandwich, 23
Taco Vegetable Soup, 24
Taco Minestrone, 24
Stuffed Pepper Soup, 25
Vegetable Beef Soup, 25
Beef Cabbage Soup, 26
Hamburger Vegetable Soup, 27
Meatball Stew, 28
Beef Barley Soup, 29
In A Hurry Beef Stew, 29
Meaty Black Bean Chili, 30
Beef Noodle Soup, 30
Cheesy Mac Chili, 31
Mexican Vegetable Soup, 31
Homemade Beef Vegetable Soup, 32

Chicken & Turkey Soups & Sandwiches

Baked Turkey Southwest Sandwiches, 34
Turkey Pancetta Sandwiches, 34
Smoked Turkey Monte Cristo Sandwiches, 35
Waldorf Turkey Sandwiches, 35
Cheesy Garlic Chicken Sandwiches, 36
Grilled Barbecue Chicken Sandwiches, 36
Open Face Buffalo Chicken Sandwiches, 37
Chicken Cheddar Wraps, 37
Buffalo Chicken Wraps, 38
Pepper Chicken Pita Wraps, 39
Salsa Ranch Chicken Wraps, 40
Guacamole Chicken Wraps, 40
Chicken Spinach Panini, 41
Jerked Chicken Sandwiches, 41
Turkey Guacamole Subs, 42
Cherry Chicken Salad Croissants, 42
Open Face Turkey Hero Sandwiches, 43
Creamy Turkey Melt, 43
Mexican Tomato Chicken Soup, 44
Chicken Alphabet Soup, 45
Chicken Rice Tortilla Soup, 45
Homemade Chicken Rice Soup, 46
Slow Cooker Chicken Stew, 47
Chicken Broccoli Stew With Lemon Dumplings, 48
Oriental Chicken Stew, 49
Oriental Chicken Noodle Soup, 50
Country Chicken Soup, 50
Zesty Chicken Soup, 51
Chunky Chicken Noodle Soup, 52
Asian Chicken Noodle Soup, 52
Fiesta Chicken Chowder, 53
Western Chicken Chowder, 54
Creamy Chicken Vegetable Soup, 54
Chicken Gumbo Soup, 55
Chicken Asparagus Soup, 56
Chicken Soup With Potato Dumplings, 57
Buffalo Chicken Soup, 57
White Bean Chicken Chili, 58
Turkey Tortilla Soup, 59
Turkey Meatball Soup, 60
Chicken Ratatouille Stew, 60

Ham, Bacon & Pork Soups & Sandwiches

Savory Ham Wraps, 62
Deli Cristos, 62
Grilled Ham & Chicken Salad Sandwiches, 63
Cheddar Ham Breakfast Sandwiches, 63
Fried Ham and Egg Salad Sandwiches, 64
Bacon Bean Sandwiches, 64
Make Your Own Panini Bar, 65
Country Ham & Peach Panini, 66
Ham Salad Sandwiches, 67
Ham Salad Croissants, 67
Warm Ham Swiss Wraps, 68
Ham Mango Wraps, 68
Melted Avocado Club Sandwiches, 69
Grilled Sourdough Clubs, 69
Antipasto Po' Boys, 70
Prosciutto Tomato Sandwiches, 70
Prosciutto Fontina Bakes, 71
Apple Prosciutto Sandwiches, 71
Cheesy Spinach Bacon Sandwiches, 72
Egg BLT With Avocado Tomato Relish, 72
Breakfast Panini Sandwiches, 73
Egg Salad BLT's, 74
Guacamole BLT, 74
Texas Toast BLT, 75
Fresh Spinach & Bacon Sandwiches, 75
Bacon Caesar Mozzarella Panini, 76
Open Face Pork Tenderloin Sandwiches, 77
Sweet & Spicy Pork, Onion & Apple Sandwiches, 77
Pork Tenderloin Sliders, 78
Italian Sausage Sandwiches, 78
Kielbasa Supper Sandwiches, 79
Grilled Honey Mustard Brats, 79
Hearty Sausage Sandwich, 80
Asparagus Prosciutto Sandwich, 81
French Club Sandwiches, 81
Bacon and Swiss Cheese Melts, 82
Italian Stuffed Sandwich, 83
Grilled Ham & Asparagus Sandwiches, 84
Ham & Cheese Loaf, 85
Tomato, Swiss and Bacon Sandwiches, 86
Grilled Pizza Pesto Sandwiches, 86
Po Boy Loaf, 87
Italian Salami Loaf, 88
Ham Black Bean Potato Soup, 88
Ham & Bean Soup, 89
Ham Bone Split Pea Soup, 90
Cheddar Ham Soup, 91
Italian Wedding Soup, 92
Southwestern Green Chile Sausage Soup, 93
Spicy Cajun Corn Soup, 94
Sausage Bean Soup, 95
Italian Root Vegetable Soup, 96
Creamy Bacon Mushroom Soup, 97
Cheesy Bacon Corn Chowder, 98
Pancetta Cheese Tortellini Soup, 99
Stir Fried Pork Soup, 100
Spicy Pork Chili, 101

Egg & Cheese Sandwiches

Herb Cheese Sandwiches with Artichoke Salsa, 103
Deviled Egg Sandwiches, 103
Fried Egg BBQ Bacon Sandwich, 104
Garlic Bread Grilled Cheese, 105
Grilled Ham & Jack Cheese, 105
Grilled Cheese Hoagies, 106
Grilled Parmesan, Tomato & Cheese Sandwiches, 106
Grilled Pimento Cheese Sandwiches, 107
Pizza Grilled Cheese, 107
Bacon, Garlic & Onion Grilled Cheese, 108
Chicken Pepper Jack Grilled Cheese, 108
Old Fashioned Grilled Cheese, 109
Havarti Pork Grilled Cheese Sandwiches, 109
Havarti Swiss Grilled Cheese, 110
Apple Ham Grilled Cheese, 110
Strawberry Goat Cheese Grilled Cheese, 111
Pepper Jack Grilled Cheese Sandwiches, 111
Monterey Jack Cheese Soup, 112
Egg Drop Soup, 112
Cheddar Cheese Soup, 113
Beer Cheese Soup, 113
Cheese & Bacon Chowder, 114
Cheese Vegetable Chowder, 114
Cheese Tortellini Vegetable Soup, 115

Fish & Seafood Sandwiches

Shrimp Club Sandwich, 117
Open Face Shrimp Sandwiches, 117
Shrimp Salad Croissants, 118
Cajun Shrimp Sandwich, 118
Shrimp Avocado Sandwiches, 119
Garlic Tuna Melts, 120
Swiss Tuna Melts, 120
Mediterranean Tuna Salad Sandwiches, 120
Tuna Burgers, 121
Veggie Tuna Burgers, 122
Herb Tuna Sandwiches, 122
Tuna Cheese Sandwiches, 123
Tuna Salad Sandwiches, 123
Garlic Shrimp Po' Boys, 124
Curried Tuna Apple Sandwiches, 124
Grilled Salmon Sandwiches, 125
Grilled Fish Sandwiches, 126
Fried Grouper Sandwiches, 127
Whitefish Reuben Sandwiches, 128
Oyster Submarine Sandwich, 129
Crab Patties, 130
Fried Oyster Po' Boys, 131
Spinach Oyster Sandwiches, 132
Open Face Crab Tomato Sandwiches, 133
Crab Salad Croissants, 133
Open Face Crab Sandwiches, 134
Crab Salad Croissants, 133
Open Face Crab Sandwiches, 134
Seafood Salad Pitas, 134
Oyster Corn Chowder, 135
Salmon Corn Chowder, 135
Halibut Chowder, 136
Shrimp Vegetable Chowder, 137
Cajun Shrimp Soup, 138

Meatless Soups & Sandwiches

Vegetable Melt, 140
Caribbean Quesadillas, 141
Bean Quesadillas, 142
Mushroom & Onion Reubens, 142
Garden Vegetable Quesadillas, 143
Baked Eggplant Sandwiches, 144
Antipasto Salad Hoagies, 145
Texas Toast Tomato Sandwiches, 145
Mexican Fiesta Loaf, 146
Grilled Vegetable Sandwiches, 147
Open Face Eggplant Sandwiches, 148
Zesty Vegetable Wraps, 148
Grilled Open Faced Summer Sandwiches, 149
Big Veggie Sandwiches, 149
Vegetable Pita Sandwiches, 150
Veggie Pockets, 150
Roasted Vegetable Sandwiches, 151
Veggie Burgers, 152
Grilled Garlic Vegetable Sandwiches, 152
Goat Cheese Roasted Red Pepper Loaf, 153
Three Cheese Tomato Melt, 153
Veggie Delight Sandwiches, 154
Fried Green Tomato Sandwiches, 155
Fried Green Tomato Po' Boys, 156
Basil Red Pepper Sandwiches, 157
Pear Waldorf Pitas, 157
Spicy Minestrone, 158
Italian Tomato Soup, 158
Cream Of Cabbage Soup, 159
Tomato Soup With Herb Croutons, 160
Basil Tomato Soup, 161
Fresh Tomato Soup, 161
Yellow Tomato Soup With Goat Cheese Croutons, 162
Chunky Tomato Vegetable Soup, 163
Cream Of Vegetable Soup, 163
Creamy Vegetable Soup, 164
Roasted Root Vegetable Soup, 165
Ultimate Veggie Soup, 166
Vegetarian Stew, 167
Roasted Vegetable Chili, 168
Meatless 5 Can Chili, 168
Weekday Vegetable Soup, 169
Cream Of Asparagus Soup, 169
Corn And Zucchini Queso Chowder, 170
Baked Potato Soup, 171

Meatless Soups & Sandwiches cont'd

Spinach Potato Soup, 171
Rustic Potato Soup, 172
Spinach Soup, 172
Broccoli Chowder, 173
Fiesta Soup, 173
Refried Bean Soup, 174
Red Lentil Soup, 174
Hearty Lentil Soup, 175
Spiced Butternut Soup, 176
Butternut Thyme Squash Soup, 177
Butternut Squash Soup, 178
Tomato Red Pepper Soup, 178
Smoky Red Pepper Soup, 179
Cheese Tortellini Tomato Soup, 180
Cheese Tortellini Garden Soup, 181
Roasted Red Pepper Soup, 182
Roasted Yellow Pepper Soup, 183
Cream Of Broccoli Soup, 184
Rosemary Mushroom Soup, 184
Cream Of Mushroom Soup, 185
Mushroom Bisque, 185
Portobello Ratatouille, 186
Speedy Tortilla Soup, 186
Mushroom Barley Soup, 187
Southwestern Soup, 187
Black Bean Soup, 188
Cream Of Roasted Garlic Soup, 189
Pumpkin Soup With Red Pepper Relish, 190
Pepper Gazpacho, 191
Spanish Gazpacho, 191
Creamy Cucumber Soup, 192
Cream Of Carrot Soup, 192
Chilled Carrot Soup, 193
Tomato Basil Bisque, 193
Leek Soup, 194
Weekday Cauliflower Soup, 194
Ramen Corn Chowder, 195
Corn Chowder, 195
Chilled Red Pepper Soup, 196
Chilled Berry Soup, 196
Strawberry Soup, 197
Cold Peach Soup, 197
Chilled Melon Soup, 198
Chilled Cantaloupe Soup, 198
Chilled Fruit Soup, 199

Cold Peach Strawberry Soup, 199

ABOUT THE AUTHOR

Lifelong southerner who lives in Bowling Green, KY. Priorities in life are God, family and pets. I love to cook, garden and feed most any stray animal that walks into my yard. I love old cookbooks and cookie jars. Huge NBA fan who loves to spend hours watching basketball games. Enjoy cooking for family and friends and hosting parties and reunions. Can't wait each year to build gingerbread houses for the kids.

CPSIA information can be obtained
at www.ICGtesting.com
Printed in the USA
LVHW100958030520
654904LV00004B/751